Transcendent

Also by Curtis White

NONFICTION

Monstrous Possibility: An Invitation to Literary Politics

The Middle Mind: Why Americans Don't Think for Themselves

*The Spirit of Disobedience: Resisting the Charms of Fake Politics,
Mindless Consumption, and the Culture of Total Work*

The Barbaric Heart: Faith, Money, and the Crisis of Nature

*The Science Delusion: Asking the Big Questions
in a Culture of Easy Answers*

We, Robots: Staying Human in the Age of Big Data

*Living In A World That Can't Be Fixed:
Reimagining Counterculture Today*

FICTION

Heretical Songs

Metaphysics in the Midwest

The Idea of Home

Anarcho-Hindu

Memories of My Father Watching TV

Requiem

America's Magic Mountain

Lacking Character

Transcendent

**art and dharma
in a time of collapse**

CURTIS WHITE

MELVILLE HOUSE
BROOKLYN • LONDON

Transcendent: Art and Dharma in a Time of Collapse

First published in 2023 by Melville House
Copyright © Curtis White 2022
All rights reserved
First Melville House Printing: November 2022

Melville House Publishing
46 John Street
Brooklyn, NY 11201
and
Melville House UK
Suite 2000
16/18 Woodford Road
London E7 0HA

mhpbooks.com
@melvillehouse

ISBN: 978-1-61219-994-8
ISBN: 978-1-61219-995-5 (eBook)

Library of Congress Control Number: 2022944576

Designed by Betty Lew

Printed in the United States of America
1 3 5 7 9 10 8 6 4 2

A catalog record for this book
is available from the Library of Congress

For Wendy,
with thanks for the Dharma Gate

Contents

Here in America we cannot define Zen Buddhists the same way we do in Japan. . . . I think you are special people and want some special practice that is not exactly priests' practice and not exactly laymen's practice. You are on your way to discovering some appropriate way of life.

—*Shunryū Suzuki*

Prologue: The Hard Problem of Art

∽

I.

I was recently listening to Father John Misty's first album *Fear Fun* on Spotify, and I noticed something that intrigued me. The songs I liked best were by a wide margin the favorite songs of many millions of other listeners. "Nancy From Now On" had fifty-two million listens. "Hollywood Forever Cemetery Sings" had forty million listens. But most other tracks on the album had only four to seven million listens. So I asked myself, "Why is that?" Not "Why do the songs have different counts" but "Why am I in such complete agreement with millions of other listeners about what the most-worthy songs are on this album?"

Perhaps it's that the songs with smaller numbers are a reflection of how many people have listened to the entire album straight through, and that the staggeringly larger numbers represent repeat listens—many repeat listens. These songs are on "heavy rotation." They are algorithmic hits. So, I wondered, "What is it about those songs that makes people want to listen to them again and again?" Ordinarily, we might explain it by simply saying they're "better" or that we "love that song so much!" Or we might say, as many a music reviewer will, that they are the "best cuts," as if that explains something. Or we avoid the problem by believing these numbers don't reveal anything other than the arid fact that, for a short while, the songs "trended" or "went viral" or were "shared" on many playlists, a regular contagion of enthusiasm that is otherwise meaningless, a mere epiphenomenon of the digital age.

Or could it be the more complicated idea that those songs are more popular because of neurology? That quite on their own, our brains experience major keys as positive and energetic, and minor keys or flatted keys like Db as introspective and sad, and a few of Misty's songs just happen to hit the neurotransmitter sweet spot. And so the skillful manipulation of major and minor keys—from which The Beatles crafted song after song, as in "I'll Cry Instead," which moves so cunningly between G-major and a B-minor bridge—can produce a song that has been enjoyed for half a century and counting. In other words, the popularity of certain songs is only about a sort of biological demagoguery, our neural wiring saying, "You *will* like this song," a pleasure pill provided courtesy of dopamine. Maybe that's what we mean when we say, "That song is dope, man."

Or is it possible to say there is something mysterious happening within music, including popular music, something that surpasses easy understanding? Is it that "Hollywood Cemetery" has soul? Does it have what Jack Kerouac called *"IT,"* the ineffable, unknowable, unnameable moment in a sax solo where the jazz soars, finds a certain note and holds it, hoping never to let go? Is it that this quality of *IT* unites us all somehow and that this unity is reflected even in Spotify's debased number-chasing? Why does it feel to us that listening to this music is not something that we *do*, but something that *happens* to us? In which case, it's not about numbers or brain chemistry at all. It's about Chuck Berry's Dionysian roustabout song "Rock and Roll Music": dancing, drinking from wooden cups, listening to my man wail on the sax, everybody shook up. Or consider the experience of singers in a gospel choir. There's nothing mysterious in their singing. It's right there. The choir feels that spirit moving through it and they're right—it is spirit welling up, spilling over, and put into our laps.

These are questions classical musicians and composers take seriously, too. I once had a conversation with Bill Cutter, composer and choral director at MIT. He pointed out that the big question is: *How do we know that the acknowledged masters of classical music—Bach in particular—are better than other equally skillful but "minor" composers?* Tartini is very good, Scarlatti is better, but Bach seems to have discovered the resonant secret to musical meaning. But how do we know Bach is better? And what do we mean by better?

This is the problem the poet Robert Browning riddled in his dramatic monologue about the Renaissance painter Andrea del Sarto. Del Sarto was a superior technician, but he envied Rafael because he reached "a heaven that's shut to me." Del Sarto was *il miglior fabbro*, the better technician, while Rafael "was flaming out his thoughts/Upon a palace-wall for Rome to see." What del Sarto couldn't understand was the *flame*, like the flame emerging from the head of a Thai Buddha. All he got for his efforts was a beautiful woman with expensive tastes who distracted him from anything blazing.

Like Browning, Cutter wondered about our "emotional response to music when no explanation for that response can be reasonably articulated." He said:

> I still cry every time I hear the second movement of the Ravel Piano Concerto in G. There is something intensely personal and profoundly sad about its meandering E major tune. No amount of musical analysis can address this. . . . thank God. I'm sure you know that famous Stravinsky quote, "Music is, by its very nature, essentially powerless to express anything at all." He's right . . . and that's what's so magical and baffling!

Arnold Schoenberg—the last of the Wagnerians, and the first of the modernists—agreed with Cutter and Stravinsky in writing: "Music does not express the extra-musical," but he added, "the composer conceives an entire composition as a spontaneous vision." But a vision of what? Not of the music as the mathematical progression of chords and rhythms, because "the composer does not . . . add bit by bit, as a child does in building with wooden blocks." For

Schoenberg, music is not in any way a mechanism, although it may be for the individual musician, busily counting and watching the conductor's baton. For Schoenberg, musicians may be artists, but the composer is a *creator*, with all of the suggestions of divinity that word implies.[1]

And so the question remains: How do we know that, for example, Gustav Mahler was better than other composers? What is it that we hear in his music that is "better"? And how was it that, fallen though the world he lived in certainly was, somehow *they*—the vague, massive public—*knew* that Mahler's music took them somewhere they'd never been before, somewhere that felt like their lives had been illuminated? Even more confusing, Mahler was a Jew. Anti-Semitic Vienna didn't want to like the Jew, so why did it? What did the Viennese hear in him?

As Mahler knew quite thoroughly, the privileged audiences that came to his concerts only wanted to be seen among those who should be seen and maybe entertained a little. So how did they know that Mahler was the One, *der Mahler*? Why did they pass Mahler along to future people more or less like themselves, worldly people, people proud in their delusions, often cruel people? Why did they know that Mahler was more important than their prejudices, their sensuality, and their vanity?

It reminds me of a story about Paul McCartney visiting Dustin Hoffman back in the day. Paul was playing guitar and composing the song "Picasso's Last Words," and Hoffman gasped, "Look, he's *doing* it! He's doing it!"

But what was he doing? And what was the "it"?

II.

These experiences and the questions that follow them are the rough equivalent of what philosophers of science call "the hard problem of consciousness." Just as consciousness cannot be reduced to mechanical structures and chemistry, the experience of Beethoven's *Great Fugue*, say, cannot be reduced to the sum of its parts—the brain is clearly involved, but it's not all about the brain.[2]

Worse yet for the neurological approach to music, it is easy to see the importance of consciousness for living things—the evolutionary advantage is obvious. But the evolutionary advantage of music is not at all clear. All of the arts obey what philosopher Hans Vaihinger called "the law of the preponderance of the means over the end." Beethoven's late string quartets are in excess of any evolutionary end or any utilitarian purpose, even the purpose of pleasure, and that's their miracle and their importance. That excess is "the hard problem of art." We wouldn't want to live in a world without art's excesses, but we have no idea why that's so.

Few critics have tried to theorize this "hard problem," but there is one effort worthy of note: screenwriter/director Paul Schrader's *Transcendental Style in Film: Ozu, Bresson, Dreyer.* The book is so good and so approachable that it should have stimulated a cottage industry in transcendental studies, but it didn't. But young Paul Schrader, just graduated from film studies in the early 1970s, dove in because, "I was curious. That curiosity grew. I realized I was far too young to write such a book. But I also realized that nobody else was writing it." The book has maintained its relevance over the last half century and was reprinted in 2018 with a new introduction, "Rethinking Transcendental Style."

Schrader argues that there are three movements in transcendental style. The first he calls the "everyday," but he doesn't mean anything sunny by the word. The everyday is the problem. It is what Buddhism calls *samsara*, the world of suffering and change, the causes and conditions into which we are born and through which we must find our way. In Japanese director Yasujirō Ozu's films, the everyday is the world of business, of office work, a Western world painfully imposed upon traditional Japanese values. Many of his male characters are "salary men," low-ranking office workers who sacrifice their male dignity and kowtow to their bosses. Schrader writes:

> In some films, such as *Early Spring*, the office "family" replaces the household family unit. Ozu focuses on the tensions between the home and the office, the parent and the child, which are extensions of the tensions between the old and new Japan, between tradition and Westernization, and—ultimately—between man and nature.

This world is, as Herbert Marcuse wrote, "a reality in which all logic and all speech are false to the extent that they are part of a mutilated whole." That's the everyday. A mutilated whole.

The second movement in transcendental style is "disparity": "a growing crack in the dull surface of everyday reality." In conventional narrative terms, the everyday is the "ground situation" and disparity is "complication," a tension created by dissatisfaction with the everyday. Ozu's salary men may be shameful in the eyes of their children, but they are at least aware that they are "bootlickers," as one father says, and capable of change and redemption (or of drinking themselves insensible). Disparity is the reason for a potentially redeeming introspection:

> If a human being can have true and tender feelings within an unfeeling environment, then there must necessarily be a disparity between man and environment. If the environment is unfeeling, where do man's feelings come from?

Introspection leads to "an outburst of spiritual emotion totally inexplicable within the everyday." Schrader calls this the moment of "decisive action." Through it, the viewer participates in the discovery that "there exists a deep ground of compassion and awareness which man and nature can touch intermittently," the transcendent.

The third movement in transcendental style is "stasis," the Wholly Other—"a frozen view of life that does not resolve the disparity but transcends it." But in what sense does it transcend? This is a messy problem for both Ozu's films and Schrader's theory.

Schrader takes one example of stasis from Ozu's *Late Spring* (1949), made in the years immediately after the war. The plot involves a young woman, Noriko (played by the superb Setsuko Hara), happily living with and caring for her father. She is pushed by her aunt and father into an arranged marriage that she doesn't want because, simply, she doesn't want to leave her father. Her selflessness and loyalty to her father is like a samurai's loyalty to his lord. According to *Hagakure, the Book of the Samurai*, the samurai has these virtues: "In terms of one's lord, loyalty; in terms of one's parents, filial piety; in martial affairs, bravery . . ."

When she is told that she can no longer serve her father/lord, she feels as if she no longer exists. To see her in her wedding gown, caught within the binding swathes of brightly colored cloth, and to see her pale, painted face in the ribboned *tsunokakushi* wig and headdress, is to see her swallowed by an alien world, when what she wanted was to be loyal, as if she were practicing *Bushido*, the samurai code of honor.

In the film's most memorable scene, Ozu offers a still life view of a vase that "connotes Oneness." Schrader writes:

> This vase is stasis, a form which can accept deep, contradictory emotion and transform it into an expression of something unified, permanent, transcendent.

Ozu keeps the camera on the vase, posed like a visitation from another world, for two long takes of six and ten seconds. To make sure that the spiritual point isn't missed, he then cuts to a lingering shot of a stately Zen rock garden next to which the father sits chatting with an old friend, neither noticing anything transcendental about the place.

In Schrader's view, this is Ozu's moment of Zen *mono no aware*, "resigned sadness," a knowing but stoic submission to the mutilations of the everyday. Unfortunately, this definition is not accurate. *Mono no aware* is not about "accepting suffering" but "awareness of impermanence," a fundamental Buddhist principle. It is a gentle sadness and not what we witness in the movie: an agony brought on by a culture's indifference to human need.

To make matters worse, Schrader thinks of the vase and the transcendent in general as "wholly other," wholly otherworldly. But from a Buddhist perspective, this is a mystification because the transcendental is not out there, solitary and apart from us save in moments of illumination. For Buddhism the transcendental is the world as we know it rightly seen. We don't need the magic of otherworldly realms because, as Zen master Shunryū Suzuki explains, the world is its own magic. The secular is the sacred, which makes Ozu's vase a golden calf.

These errors aside, we ought to wonder, "Who is this moment-of-the-vase for?" It can't be for Noriko because she is lying on the floor on a futon and doesn't see the vase. So, obviously, it must be Ozu and his audience who are seeing it, and if there is transcendence being offered, it is offered to himself and to us, not to the characters in the drama. The characters are not self-aware; they are like the conventional figures in the performance of Noh Theater that Noriko and her father attend earlier in the film. In an odd way, the vase is a happy ending for Ozu and his audience, but not for Noriko.

Schrader believes that the vase represents Zen values, but that is not the only possible interpretation. At the time he was making this film, Ozu, like most Japanese people, was coming to terms with his complicity with the Japanese war machine, so deeply rooted in the traditions of samurai stoicism. (The *Hagakure* instructs samurais, "If one were to say what it is to do good, in a single word it would be to endure suffering.") Ozu, too, once bowed to Japan's warrior cult, as revealed in his disturbing 1932 film *I Was Born, But . . .* The film presents itself as a comedy about childhood, a coming-of-age tale, but it is also a prophetic wish for an industrialized Japanese nationalism that was beginning to assert itself, much to the world's horror. Nearly all critics of the film imagine it is a charming and light comedy, but I think it is an elegant, beautifully realized work of propaganda that argues that Western industrialism and business culture are acceptable only so long as they are subservient to the Japanese martial spirit. Ozu offers this ominous yearning as childhood's wisdom.

The difficulty in understanding Ozu's intentions in *Late Spring* is the difficulty in knowing whether the vase represents Zen enlightenment or samurai stoicism, or a confusion of the two. Historically, samurai culture adopted Zen because it believed that Zen offered warriors composure on the battlefield, stoicism in the face of death, and superior battle skills in sword fighting and archery—just as a modern sports psychologist might teach meditation to a baseball pitcher in order to improve his performance on the mound. (Seventeenth-century Zen monk Takuan Sōhō wrote several theses on swordsmanship: "When killing there is no thought of killing.") In other words, samurai culture thought it was getting something from Zen practice, but as Shunryū Suzuki wrote in *Zen Mind, Beginner's Mind*, "If you think you will get something from practicing zazen, already you are involved in impure practice."[3]

There is a third option: perhaps the vase is more like one of Alfred Hitchcock's "MacGuffins." It's an object pregnant with meaning that is finally meaningless. It's like the monolith in Kubrick's *2001: A Space Odyssey*; it is a narrative device. It pretends to have transcendental meaning, but it is really only a pretext for adventures in space travel with a compromised computer system named HAL. If I'm right to suggest this, the vase also means that Ozu was a clever filmmaker, which he certainly was.[4]

Which brings me back to Schrader's book. What Schrader is finally interested in is not eternity but artifice, which for him means cinematic technique. The 2018 introduction to his 1971 book makes this clear because he now situates transcendental style in the context of many styles employed by filmmakers in the "slow cinema" movement, like Robert Bresson's *Pickpocket* (1959) and Béla Tarr's astonishing seven-hour *Sátántangó* (1994). The transcendental is just one strategy among many—including static frame, wide angles, offset edits, etc.—that were made available to directors after cinema's turn to the "long take." (Ozu's vase is shown in two long takes.) The use of transcendental style may suggest something spiritual but that's not required. It's only that the style is available when needed in order to provide the aroma of the otherworldly, whether the artist is sincere about it or not. It is the style that matters, not the eternity. It's a technique.

Which is fine. I learned a lot about slow cinema from Schrader's new introduction. But transcendence is no longer his point and probably wasn't from the first.

III.

In this work, however, I am indeed interested in the spiritually transcendent because I'm interested in the way in which certain works of art, works to which we seem to humanly gravitate, suggest an inexpressible meaningfulness that can't be reduced to brain chemistry or a trick of the artist's trade. I will not try to explain what can't be expressed, but I would like to remember that its presence in our lives is real even if it can't be entirely explained. As Rōshi Robert Aitken suggested of Zen, "Our practice is not to clear up the mystery. It is to make the mystery clear."

I am also interested in a much more concrete form of transcendence, social transcendence, rising above "dark karma," what Buddhism calls "the causes and conditions" of the world that we are born into. In karma (for us, the late capitalist social order), we are alienated from nature and from our own human nature by what is customary. The Buddha taught this and so did Marx, Nietzsche, and even the sixteenth-century essayist Michel de Montaigne who wrote, "Custom is the most powerful master of all things."

> Little by little and stealthily, she establishes within us the footing of her authority; but having, by this mild and humble beginning, stayed and rooted it with the aid of time, she then displays a fierce and

tyrannical countenance, in opposition to which we
no longer have liberty even to lift up our eyes. We
see her do violence constantly to the laws of nature.

The point for Buddhism is to stop perpetuating karma/cul-
ture, our social fate, and to go *beyond* it, into an alternative
social reality, the Sangha community. Western art has had a
similar purpose. As early as Andreas Mantegna (1431–1506),
art set about the problem not only of visual perspective but of
social perspective, seeing itself not sunk within the reigning
political order but perched outside of that order, judging it,
and declaring its independence. Karma/culture is enchantment, and art and Dharma have as a common goal our *dis-
enchantment*. (See my reading of Mantegna's "The Gonzaga
Family" in "Boss Trump: Capitalism Gone Wild.")

Obviously, these two ways of thinking about transcendence are related: to whatever degree we can transcend
karma/culture, to that degree we can begin to discover what
it might mean to live in connection with our true nature.
This is the dialectic between "freedom from" and "freedom
to." This is the secret meaning of all countercultures, and
it is entirely ordinary and nothing mystical. For instance,
when the post-punk band Sonic Youth played "Hendrix
Necro" and Kim Gordon sang, "I want to *be free,*" they were
saying the obvious ("I want to be free from a corporate culture of death-in-life") and the not so obvious ("I want to
be free to live *beyond* that culture"). Far from being nihilistic, punk is the transcendental aspiration of people living in
an utterly damaged world who are (rather loudly) seeking

their happiness. That is not something true only in a long-passed punk era, it is true in the present as the neo-punk band Idles reveals: the right to happiness is the living edge of their music (the title of their first album is "Joy as an Act of Resistance").[5] The crudeness of punk music is actually an aesthetic: "If I must live in a dead world, I'll be deader than death, and thus live." Or as Buddhism expresses it, "We must become dead to death in order to be free." Punk, too, is the expression of a desire to awaken.

Awakening through art and awakening to Dharma, the wisdom of "what is," may not be the same, but they are deeply compatible. As Jorge Luis Borges imagined:

> We (the indivisible divinity operating within us) have dreamt the world. We have dreamt it as firm, mysterious, visible, ubiquitous in space and durable in time, but in its architecture we have allowed tenuous and eternal crevices of unreason which tell us it is false.

Note that Borges writes that it is the divinity within us that wakens from the dreamwork of reality. The next question is, of course, "What is this divinity?" Borges provides an answer, but he does so implicitly. What is beyond our shared hallucination of reality is the poem. This passage is from a prose piece, one of Borges's *ficciones*, but it is poetry in a deeper sense. Like Dharma, it is language opening up to "what is." As the *Heart Sutra* explains, there is form (ubiquitous in space and durable in time), and there is emptiness (the realization that form is a dream). We need the dream of form, but we also need to know that the dream is a dream. Not to know that is to proceed in delusion.

As for myself, I am not a Dharma teacher or a scholar of Eastern religions. I won't even say that I am a Buddhist because I don't know what it means to say, "I am a Buddhist." The phrase seems to me to be self-contradictory: too much "I" and too much "it." To say "I am a Buddhist" tends to reify Buddhism and to make it thing-like, in spite of the fact that it is a spiritual tradition for which reification is something like original sin. All I can say is that I am "on the path," and a long, strange path it has been.

This path opened for me in the early 1980s when I visited my sister Wendy's apartment in San Francisco, corner of Oak and Page, right across the street from the famed San Francisco Zen Center and a block from Tassajara's Green Gulch Grocer, where I bought my morning granola. Wendy and her husband Van Vorheis (now the ordained master Kelsang Tsogtor) were members of the Zen community and took me to Dharma talks at the Center. They also had a shelf of books about Buddhism that I plundered happily, including Tarthang Tulku's *Time, Space, and Knowledge: A New Vision of Reality* (1977), a book that suggested to me that Buddhism had a deconstructive soul.

These happy accidents didn't change the course of my life; I remained an essayist/novelist/professor. I didn't go to India or Thailand or live in a monastery. It was enough that

Dharma helped me and changed me when I needed help and I needed to change. What changed was not the course of my life but my life's ground. Dharma gave me a place to stand.

Intellectually, what first attracted me to Buddhism was the similarity of its concept of "emptiness" to certain Western philosophies, especially those of Nietzsche and Jacques Derrida. (Yes, I confess, I entered Buddhism at its deep end.) Derrida's concept of deconstruction shows that the Ego, His Majesty the Sovereign Self, is nothing in itself but exists only by being "supplemented" by what is not the self. Similarly for Buddhism, the self has no self-existence (*anātman*); the self is present only through those things that are not self.

In a famous story, King Milinda asks the sage Nagasena about non-self. The sage explains that there is no Nagasena, that his name is only a sound. To illustrate, Nagasena asks the king to consider his chariot. Is the chariot its axle, its wheel, or the reins? There is no chariot-in-itself. Each of the things that supplement the chariot can in their turn be broken down into parts—wood, iron, leather, etc.—and those are made of trees, water, sunshine, and minerals. In Thich Naht Hahn's phrase, things like King Milinda and his chariot don't have self-existence, they "inter-are."

Beyond the intriguing similarity between deconstruction and emptiness, I learned there was an ethical depth to Buddhism, a clarity about how to live, that was sorely lacking in Derrida's work and generally underdeveloped in Western philosophy. And yet even as my spiritual interests drifted from the West to the East, I also came to see that in its own redeeming way, Western art and philosophy had been working slowly and haltingly toward Dharma for the last two-and-a-half centuries, something I will explain in detail in "Beyond the Database Buddha."

While I'm making confessions, I ought also to say that I am not a musicologist, an art historian, a literary scholar, an economist, a philosopher, or a film critic. I am expert in nothing. I am a beginner in all things. But I take comfort in Shunryū Suzuki's words: "In the beginner's mind there are many possibilities; in the expert's mind there are few. . . . This is the real secret of the arts: always be a beginner."

I.

Delusion

It's only because of their stupidity that they're able to be so sure of themselves.

—*Kafka,* The Trial

Beyond the Database Buddha

For Donald Wolff and Allen Dunn

౦౦

A periwinkle that stood near him and whose
blue gaze he had already met a number of times,
touched him now from a more spiritual distance,
but with so inexhaustible a meaning that it
seemed as if there were nothing more that could
be concealed. . . . He had passed over to the other
side of Nature.

—*Rainer Maria Rilke,* "An Experience"

I.

Western Buddhism has two truly fundamental questions
about its relationship to Eastern Buddhism. The first is a
productive question that can be posed in multiple ways:
Why has the West been so open to Buddhist thought and
practice? Why does Buddhism feel so *familiar*, part of the
family, somehow always already a portion of who we are?
Why does it seem at times as if Buddhism is something that
has *returned* to us? This is an uncanny but fruitful question.

The second question is more troubling. In what ways have

we distorted Buddhism because we have tried to understand it through our own ways of knowing? Particularly problematic is our tendency to understand everything, Buddhism included, in scientific terms—through empiricism, logic, and data gathering. This tendency has been present since the great scientific revolutions of the nineteenth and early twentieth centuries, but it is intensely present in the techno-capitalist world of the present. We should be asking, "At what point do scientific investigations turn Buddhism into a mere/mirror reflection of the science investigators?"[1] Is an empirical and secular Buddhism just another example of cultural appropriation? Or is it more like what Thomas Kuhn called a "paradigm shift" in which the basic "normal" assumptions about Buddhism are transformed into something superior: a scientific Buddha?[2]

One thing these questions suggest is the idea that there is no "normative" Buddhism. There is no *one* Buddhism, only Buddhist "ecologies."[3] Buddhist teaching and practice is always influenced by local histories, cultures, and conventions, as well as by extrinsic influences like that of Western culture on Asian cultures. And so Eastern Buddhist Dharma and meditation practices have been joined to our own ways of knowing, creating not only a scientific Buddha but also a corporate Buddha, a self-help Buddha, and a scholarly Buddha, as well as the "purer" Buddha found in Zen or Vipassana centers like the Zen Center in San Francisco and Spirit Rock Meditation Center in Marin, California.

Some of these ecologies threaten the coherence of Buddhist practice, but corporate Buddhism poses a particular threat. Witness Amazon's 2021 project AmaZen, a small booth (a "despair closet," as some have called it) installed in distribution warehouses where employees can go to "focus on their mental wellbeing." As Robert Raymond writes:

> Amazon's WorkingWell program is just part of a much broader trend taking place throughout the corporate landscape encouraging workers to utilize activities such as yoga, meditation and mindfulness to reduce work-related stress and improve performance.[4]

The difference between these ecologies is that while corporate Buddhism—like Google's Search Inside Yourself program—has made accommodations with a larger materialist and consumerist culture, the purer Buddhist ecologies have remained if not dissident at least different from that larger culture. That is so because Zen, in particular, became broadly accessible in the West during a period of remarkable open possibility, what we now call the 1960s counterculture, during which ways of thinking and living were considered that only a few years earlier would have seemed utterly alien to Western sensibilities. It was another of those rare moments in which people felt permitted to engage imaginatively with alternative ways of thinking and being. As the Reverend Dr. Kenneth Tanaka suggests:

> [In the 1960s], Buddhism [came] to be seen less as a weird "Oriental" cult. . . . In fact, as the number of

people interested in spiritual matters increased, it was often thought, however naively, that "spiritual Asia" was superior to the "materialistic West."[5]

There was nothing strange in our counterculture's attraction to Buddhism because, as Robert Thurman observed in *Essential Tibetan Buddhism* (1995), Buddhism itself is "a countercultural movement that endured." The monastic organization was a kind of inversion of the military organization: a peace army rather than a war army, a self-conquest tradition rather than an other-conquest tradition, a science of inner liberation rather than a science of liberating the outer world from the possession of others.

By the early 1960s, just about every aspect of North American culture had been safely secularized for the benefit of the postwar, postindustrial world of business and its crowds of men in "grey flannel suits." But in the later 1960s, two untoward things—the counterculture and Zen Buddhism— fell from the sky and they were unapologetically not secular, not about business, and not predictable. From the perspective of the corporate culture of that time and our own, the counterculture and its alien religions were in urgent need of secularization and, brother, that was swiftly on the way. Zen and other Eastern religions like the Krishna Consciousness Movement (1966) needed to be *managed*. All that was required was an inspirational manager, and then, as if on cue, along came Steve Jobs and his omnivorous creation, the Apple I microcomputer (1976).

Jobs adapted both Zen and the counterculture to the purposes of a cutthroat corporate monopoly. (Co-opting the
name of The Beatles' production company, Apple, in the
process.) The burgeoning tech industry took it from there.
They not only neutralized the counterculture and Zen as
threats to their ideological dominance, they used them for
the purposes of branding: they became *marketing* tools—
"Think different!" Worse yet, tech made Zen coexten-
sive with something capitalism was perfectly comfortable
with—the science of mindfulness! As Google's Search Inside
Yourself Institute now loudly declares: BORN AT GOOGLE AND
BASED ON NEUROSCIENCE.

Tanaka is correct to think that the years of the counterculture provided Buddhism with an opportunity to natu-
ralize in the West, but he does not ask what it was *within*
the counterculture that made it so receptive. The answer,
I would suggest, is that the West had already been prepar-
ing for Buddhism's arrival through dissident cultures in the
arts, music, literature, and philosophy as far back as the late
eighteenth century. The counterculture found inspiration
for alternative ways of living in psychedelic music, avant-
garde jazz, color-filled pop art, *vers libre* poetry, and black
humor novelists like Richard Brautigan, Kurt Vonnegut,
and Joseph Heller. These art scenes hearkened directly back
to Romanticism's anarchic tradition of nonconformity: the
poet visionary, the dandy, the bohemian, the mystic, and the
utopian, misfits all.[6]

For anyone who has ever listened to one of Jerry Garcia's
extended guitar improvisations with the Grateful Dead, even

without Owsley's chemical enhancements, the idea that the counterculture was open to transcendence is no news. And then along came Zen, right up Oak Street from the Haight. As The Animals sang in 1965, "We Gotta Get Out of This Place." Buddhism appeared as a consoling and virtuous place to get to, certainly better than Vietnam or stacked up in offices with the white shirts and power ties. It was a place not yet corrupted by the West's restless materialism.

Because of Western Buddhism's roots in the counterculture, it has not become legalistic or dogmatic; it has remained open to and tolerant of Buddhist variants following Zen master Dogen's assurance that there can be "seven sweet dumplings and five savory dumplings," but the heart of the Dharma remains the same. The question is, does secular/ scientific Buddhism accept this? Or does it mean to foreclose on Buddhism's openness? Is it a form of spiritual colonialism meant to limit the number of dumplings on offer to one?

The tendency to narrow and foreclose is present in professional journals in Buddhist studies like the *Journal of the International Association of Buddhist Studies,* or the online *Journal of Global Buddhism (JGB).* These journals find it difficult to resist the gravitational pull of mathematics and empiricism. As *JGB* announces on its website: "The journal will function as an independent research tool itself, emphasizing surveys, the creation of databases, empirical investigations, and through the presentation of ongoing research projects." [sic]

As B. Alan Wallace writes in *Buddhism & Science: Breaking New Ground* (2003):

Buddhism, like science, presents itself as a body of systematic knowledge about the natural world, and it posits a wide array of testable hypotheses and theories concerning the nature of the mind and its relation to the physical environment. . . . Buddhism may be better characterized as a form of empiricism rather than transcendentalism.

Although Wallace is critical of the crude materialism of so-called "secular Buddhism," he has used the assumption of the ultimate compatibility of Buddhism and science to create the Santa Barbara Institute for Consciousness Studies, which describes itself in this way:

Nature and potential of human consciousness: Exploring the fundamental questions about the origins, nature, and potentials of consciousness by integrating the methods of inquiry of contemplatives and scientists.

For Wallace, Buddhism has a place in the West only if it is empirical and pragmatic. This is "Big Science" Buddhism, which is the only kind of research that will attract outside funding from government, corporations, or foundations. Corporate foundations are not going to fund studies of Buddhism and the arts.

And then there is Mindfulness-Based Stress Reduction (MBSR) developed in 1979 by Jon Kabat-Zinn, an MIT-trained scientist. As Kabat-Zinn has described his project: "It was always my intention that mindfulness move into the mainstream. This is something that people are now finding compelling in many countries and many cultures. The reason is the science," especially the neuroscience.

Neuroscience has been a particularly troubling player in the corporatization of Dharma. Using fMRI technology on meditators, it has sought what has been derisively called the "Buddha Spot" in the brain.[7] The primary success of this wildly expensive research has been in garnering funding for future data gathering, all with the vague hope that something will be discovered that can be offered as a therapy for "our busy, stressful modern lives." But for Buddhist scholar Bernard Faure, neuroscience's data gathering merely follows what he calls the "blind logic of accumulation."

For neuroscience, Buddhist spirituality is just another "ghost in the machine" and is incompatible with scientific thought. Its only use is to offer triage for the suffering of people immobilized in the office, stuck in traffic, in prison, or in a war zone in the Middle East. The data-phile Steven Pinker offers broad ideological support for the neuroscientists. As he argues in his book *Enlightenment Now*, the world should be seen in utilitarian terms not only because that is a more rational way to proceed, but because it is morally superior. He writes, "A quantitative mindset, despite its nerdy aura, is in fact the morally enlightened one."

The global economic infrastructure has supported Kabat-Zinn's stress reduction projects and now employs his findings in the corporate world. As Otto Scharmer wrote of the 2014 World Economic Forum in Davos, corporate mindfulness is at the tipping point. "Mindfulness practices like meditation are now used in technology companies such as Google and

Twitter (amongst others), in traditional companies in the car and energy sectors, in state-owned enterprises in China, and in UN organizations, governments, and the World Bank."[8]

Amazingly, mindfulness for stress reduction is not a uniquely Western phenomenon. In Buddhist countries like Korea, a secularized form of meditation whose purpose is to reduce the mental burden of constant work is becoming common. Some Korean teashops have developed a Buddha-lite practice of "hitting mung," or sitting without doing anything. A Seoul teashop called Green Lab recently introduced a relaxation concept that it calls, strangely, "ritual." Jung Jae-hwan, head of the skin care brand, Hyggee, said that he had been looking for ways to find peace as he hustled in an intensely competitive business world. "I wanted to be able to press the stop button and take a moment for myself, but I feel like I constantly have to do something." Of course, in times past, Jae-hwan's temple monk would have called this "agitation" and prescribed meditation and the study of Dharma, but these are modern times in which Buddhist practices arrive in historically Buddhist countries and are taken for something brand new derived from the esteemed capitalist West![9]

The problem with a utilitarian Buddha is clearly stated by David R. Loy in *Ecodharma: Buddhist Teachings for the Ecological Crisis* (2019):

A more secular, *this-worldly* [Buddhism] has become popular, especially in the West: understanding the Buddhist path more psychologically, as a new type of therapy that provides different perspectives on the nature of mental distress . . . the solution is to change the way my mind works, so that I can play my various roles (at work, with family, with friends, and so on) better—in short, so that I *fit into this world better.*

Of course, the Buddha did not seek to fit into his world better. He left it behind and sought refuge in wisdom.

The tendency in the West to make Buddhism accommodate itself to the West's empirical and pragmatic assumptions about the nature of reality has been a problem from the beginning. As the grand old man of Buddhist studies Edward Conze observed in his collection of essays *Thirty Years of Buddhist Studies* (1968):

> The study of the Mahayana sutras is either left to outsiders lodged precariously on the margin of society, or is carried on for reasons which have little to do with their actual message,—such as an interest in linguistic problems. . . .

Scholars of Buddhism, he concluded, tend to take "no living interest" in their subject, creating a Buddhism that is, in Coleridge's phrase, "varnished rather than polished." Or as Dogen wrote, "Scholars who go about counting up words are not adequate to serve as teachers and guides: they would be like the blind trying to lead the blind."[10]

Thich Naht Hahn offers a relevant anecdote. During an international conference on religion in the early 1970s, Naht Hahn asked a professor about "religious experience." The professor replied baldly:

> I don't know what you mean by religious experience. I am a professor of religion; we have things that we can think and speak of and teach on the conceptual level. I don't think that—except on the conceptual level—we have anything to exchange.[11]

For another telling example of what Conze was concerned with, there is one of the world's leading Buddhist scholars Richard Gombrich (former Boden professor of Sanskrit at Oxford and author of *What the Buddha Thought* (2009)) who cheerfully acknowledges, "I am not a Buddhist." Nothing wrong with that. However, his interest in Buddhism is significantly mediated by Karl Popper, a British philosopher of science and "critical rationalist." Following Popper, Gombrich's primary area of study is "the logical derivation of its ethics." At the same time, he dismisses Western Buddhism as a self-interested "cult of meditation." For Gombrich, Buddhism is something outside, over there, in Asia.[12]

Even so, all need not be lost. As the great Protestant theologian Paul Tillich remarked:

> The secular religions [science], like the proper religions, are open to many developments. They can be very solid expressions of ultimate concern in

secular language. That is, they can be this as long
as a religious substance remains effective in them
despite the secularization, or as long as the ultimate
concern or "infinite passion" is still in them and
shines through them.[13]

So the critical question is, does Buddhism's infinite passion
survive in secular/scientific Buddhism? If the answer to that
question is no, as I am arguing, there is still a creative opportunity for us: Is it possible to *theorize* Western Buddhism in a
different way, through the arts? The "Buddhist modernism"
of the sciences has not been bashful about its theorizing; it
has concluded that Buddhism can be safely reduced to magical thinking and brain chemistry, but it's okay if it is useful
for "human flourishing," especially in the corporate work
space. I intend to offer the possibility of an alternate Buddhist modernism, an "aesthetic education," to use Friedrich
Schiller's phrase, because the arts are not merely shiny orna-
ments for Dharma.

The arts are Heart Matter.

II.

It is very advisable to examine and dissect the
men of science for once, since they for their part
are quite accustomed to laying bold hands on
everything in the world, even the most venerable
things, and taking them to pieces.

—*Nietzsche*

Stephen Batchelor is currently the preeminent advocate of an atheist Buddhism working within a "secular age," but this has not always been the case. In his 1997 book *Buddhism Without Beliefs*, he described himself as agnostic, not atheist, saying, "An agnostic Buddhist eschews atheism as much as theism." He also considered the arts and the imagination to be at the heart of Dharma. He wrote, "Dharma practice is more akin to artistic creation than technical problem solving." In short, "The genius of the Buddha lay in his imagination."

Batchelor's perspective has changed dramatically in recent years. Science, not imagination, is now at the core of his thinking. In his most recent book, *After Buddhism: Rethinking the Dharma for a Secular Age* (2017), he writes, "The worldview of modern science provides [Buddhism] with a sound and fertile foundation." His work now shares the assumptions advanced by the science-oriented work of the New Atheist movement led by evolutionary biologist Richard Dawkins, Christopher Hitchens, cognitive psychologist Steven Pinker, and neuroscientist Sam Harris. As Hitchens wrote of Batchelor's 2010 book *Confessions of a Buddhist Atheist,* "Stephen Batchelor adds the universe of Buddhism to the many fields in which received truth and blind faith are now giving way to ethical and scientific humanism, in which lies our only real hope."

Batchelor shares another trait with the New Atheists: he wants to have it both ways. He wants a pragmatic, empirical Buddhism which reasons that if it can't have spiritual transcendence, it can still have the awe-inspiring beauties provided by science. Here is one dandy of tortured logic to prove his point: (1) Darwin wrote, "From so simple a beginning endless forms most beautiful and most wonderful have been, and are being, evolved." (2) The Buddha said, "That which the wise in the world agree upon as existing, I too say that it exists." (3) The Buddha would have agreed that Darwin was a wise man. (4) Ergo, the Buddha would have agreed with Darwin's claim that evolution is beautiful. To make matters worse, what Darwin meant by "beauty" and "wonder" is unexamined because everyone knows what beauty is. Right? This logic is straight from the New Atheist playbook: *If* inspiring beauty is needed (an open question for them), science can provide all we need without aid from the arts or religion.

Buddhist naturalists like Batchelor and Owen Flanagan (*The Boddhisattva's Brain: Buddhism Naturalized*, 2011) are appalled by the idea that in a rational culture people should be attracted to what Flanagan calls the "nonsense" of Eastern Buddhism. Flanagan wishes to imagine:

> [A] Buddhism without rebirth and without a karmic system that guarantees justice ultimately will be served, without nirvana, without Bodhisattvas flying on lotus leaves, without Buddha worlds, without nonphysical states of mind, without any deities, without heaven and hell realms, without oracles, and without lamas who are reincarnations of lamas.

But for many Buddhists, myself included, Batchelor's and Flanagan's criticism of Buddhist metaphysics is aimed at low-hanging fruit, below-the-belt low, because next to none of what they criticize has been taken literally in the West. I have a Tibetan thangka with an image of Avalokiteshvara, the bodhisattva of compassion, but that doesn't mean I think she was ever an earthly being or that I ought to worship her. Western Buddhists are free to enjoy Buddhist art and folklore and even superstition without thinking of them as a system of necessary beliefs. The art, folklore, and "nonsense" of Buddhism is part of the pleasure, the emotional depth, and the spiritual richness of trying on this untried world of experience and ideas. The nonsense is part of the point, as the English poet and Zen teacher Henry Shukman shows in a penetrating essay:

> A conjured deity travels past innumerable "buddha-worlds" to teleport a host of 84,000 bodhisattvas to Vimalakirti's hut. . . . It would be easy to gloss this as mere religious hyperbole. But it has a cumulative effect. It takes us not just to a realm of poetry, but to a condition in which our conventional understanding of the ways things work is disassembled.[14]

Stephen Batchelor is like the autobiographical narrator in Herman Melville's *Typee* who lived happily among South Sea islanders until it was time for him to be adopted into the tribe. But that required having his face tattooed. So, he demurred and returned to the West. Melville discovered the limits of cross-cultural exchange and so has Batchelor.

∞

Batchelor thinks that Buddhism can be saved from metaphysical nonsense simply by better understanding its historical origins. Much of *After Buddhism* is devoted to readings of early Pali texts that show the Buddha as a human among humans seeking not ultimate truths but, like ancient Greek philosophy, the best way to live in the here and now. As one reviewer wrote, Batchelor has discovered that "what . . . Buddhism *ought to be* in our era turns out to be what Buddhism *was* at the beginning."[15] And yet this turn to origins is something that Batchelor himself warned against in another of his early books, *The Awakening of the West* (1994):

> Much scholarly energy was taken up with a pervasive preoccupation of the 19th century: the quest for origins. This resulted by the 1870s in the Pali texts being widely accepted as earlier than the Sanskrit writings, which led to the assumption that they were therefore truer and more essential . . . which neatly supported the belief that the later a particular manifestation of Buddhism was, the more corrupt it was liable to be.

But that was then.

I'd be tempted to call Batchelor a "strict constructionist" if it weren't for the fact that some of his stricter constructions eliminate ideas that have been the bedrock of any form of Buddhism, whether East or West, for the last two-and-a-half millennia. For example, he replaces the Four Noble Truths[16] with an earlier understanding of the Buddha's thought, the Four Tasks, and he does this in spite of the fact that the

Four Noble Truths, the Middle Way, and the Eightfold Path were the very first things the Buddha taught at Deer Park, forty-nine days after his enlightenment (*Dhammacakkappavattana Sutta*). And yet Batchelor insists that, "The fundamental doctrine of Buddhism [the Four Noble Truths] was *grafted onto preexistent teachings.*" Happily for Batchelor, these earlier-than-early teachings confirm his own modern and pragmatic version of Dharma.

Batchelor argues against the Four Noble Truths not only because of their inauthenticity but also because he believes that the Truths are metaphysical—they are mere beliefs independent of experience. But the Four Noble Truths are *not* dependent on metaphysics. (Not that there is anything wrong with metaphysics, as I will explain shortly.) They are not commandments carved in stone and they were not taken from Brahmanism, as Batchelor suggests. The Buddha's pedagogy was, "Listen to what I have to say, consider what you have heard, and cultivate what seems worthy." But consider how? Consider in the light of your own experience! And if experience provides consent, then, by all means, cultivate. As Immanuel Kant directed, "Sapere aude," dare to think for yourself. The Buddha said much the same thing in his sermon to the Kalama:

> Do not be led by reports or tradition or hearsay. Be not led by the authority of religious texts . . . nor by the idea, 'this is our teacher.' But when you know for yourselves that certain things are wholesome and good, then accept them and follow them. (*Kalama Sutta*)

For most Western Buddhists, the Four Noble Truths are true not because a god or an authority said they were true, but because they agree with our experience. The idea that the world is innately unsatisfactory because people are angry and greedy, and they're angry and greedy because they are deluded, is a good rendering of our own experience in *samsara*-land, the world of suffering and change, the corporate capitalist West.

Batchelor's anti-metaphysics argues not only for "Buddhism without beliefs," it also argues for a Buddhism without a "beyond," the realm of the "supramundane." Batchelor insists that in concepts like "Buddha nature" metaphysics has once again been added to the earliest Buddhist teachings. The idea of Buddha nature is a distortion, he claims, something borrowed from the Hindu concept of *atman* (the spiritual essence in all beings). It is metaphysics and grossly inappropriate for a rational and secular age.

What this argument ignores is that the appeal to a transcendent Buddha nature is not simply metaphysical because when we make contact with it, we do so through the mundane world that we live in. As Rilke's periwinkle suggests, any sense of a beyond is always to be found in what is here. As *Tricycle* editor Andrew Cooper explains:

> When I moved to the Pacific Northwest, someone told me something that was very helpful for brightening the long, dark, rainy winters. Even during stretches when it might rain for weeks on end, there are, almost every day, small snatches of sun-

light. Over time, one comes to love them all the more for their fragile brevity. I find that the spirituality of Pure Land [Buddhism] is akin to that. It breaks through, surprisingly, through no effort of one's own, unannounced, gently, and in the small moments of life. Being seized by the world—by a passage of literature, a breath of song, a conversation with a friend, or the sun's appearance on an overcast day. . . . [17]

In this way, Cooper concludes, we don't seek Dharma "out there" in metaphysics land; we let Dharma come to us through the things of this world. Our only requirement is to be "awake" when it arrives. This is the essence of the Middle Way: not transcendental and not material but both at once. As Frederick Streng explained in *Emptiness: A Study in Religious Meaning* (1967):

The highest truth exists in dependence on everyday activities while transcending and purifying them. . . . This way of knowing is based on an ontological commitment to two spheres of reality: the "natural sphere" and the "wholly other," the latter being both transcendent to and immanent in the former.

Buddhists and artists and lovers and spiritual seekers of whatever stripe don't want their experience of the infinite explained away, they don't want the vastness of heart replaced with tasks, although they don't want to accept it blindly either.

What they would like is to understand their passion better. That is what Dharma attempts to do: help us to understand what we have always known in our mind/heart.

But wait a minute, why am I explaining the Middle Way, Buddhism 101, to the esteemed Stephen Batchelor? It is very, very strange, unless the Middle Way is, like the Four Noble Truths, one of those things we're going to have to learn to do without in the brave new world of secular Buddhism.

Like Batchelor, Western Buddhism may not be open to the dogma of personal karma leading to literal re-birth, but it doesn't have to be because the Buddha's understanding of reincarnation is actually quite subtle. As the 19th-century monk-scholar Kunzang Pelden wrote, "It is not that there is a movement or transmigration of something from a former to a subsequent state. . . . When one uses a lamp to light another lamp, the later flame cannot be lit without dependence upon the first; but at the same time, the first flame does not pass into the second one." As contemporary monk/scholar Bhikkhu Bodhi explains, ". . . rebirth can take place without the presence of a substantial self that maintains its identity as it transmigrates from one life to the next."

> Without a self to hold the sequence together, what connects one life to the next is nothing other than the principle of conditionality. Conditions in one existence initiate the arising of the conditioned phenomena in the next existence.[18]

In other words, what is "re-born" is not you, but the way you lived, your habits of mind, whether compassionate or deluded, greedy, and angry. Or perhaps the Buddha himself said it best and most directly, "Here, monks, I say there is no coming, no going, no standing still; no passing away and no being reborn." (*Udana*, Sutta 8:1)

Now we come to the heart of the matter, or the "heartwood," in the Buddha's word—the unborn, the unconditioned, the *transcendent*. Whether Batchelor thinks it metaphysical or not, Western Buddhism remains deeply invested in the idea that Buddhism offers a "refuge" that includes not only teachings and community but the promise of transcendental solace. To take a typical case, Martin Aylward, founder of the Moulin de Chaves retreat center in France, offers his students "rich Dharma teachings and valuable practices to help us understand more deeply what the traditions call Primordial Awareness . . . the Ground of Being . . . the 'natural state' or 'awareness of awareness.'" Aylward's Dharma may offend Batchelor's originalist assumptions, but it does so in the same way that advocates of a "living constitution" offend political conservatives. As Dharma teachers sometimes say of their teachings, "It is not in the sutras, but it is well established."

On the other hand, Batchelor makes it clear enough that even after his many years studying and meditating in the East, he is not interested in meditation as a means to arrive at some fanciful "awareness of awareness," what Flanagan calls "non-physical states of mind." He is not interested in what Thanissara of Sacred Mountain Sangha describes as "using the mind, to look at the mind, to go beyond the mind." The only question for Batchelor is whether a secular Buddhism, stripped of transcendental pretensions, can lead to "human flourishing." Does it provide "what appears to be an entirely adequate ethical, contemplative, and philosophical framework for leading a flourishing life in *this* world"? He seeks an "everyday sublime," although what Batchelor means, exactly, by the words "everyday" and "sublime" is not clear.

As I wrote earlier, Buddhism exists in ecologies. So, the question becomes, is secular Buddhism, shorn of the transcendent and based upon science, the most desirable Buddhist ecology? Batchelor clearly seems to think so. Nevertheless, his conclusions do nothing to change the fact that in the Western Buddhist community, there are now and will continue to be students of the Dharma who are interested in the transcendent, in Buddha nature, and in what is often called an Original Brightness or Big Mind. What does Batchelor have to say to these people other than to leave them with the unpleasant feeling that they are just gullible Westerners taken in by the mysterious East?

However, the gullible have their own questions. At the deepest level, the transcendental seeker might ask, "Why should life flourish?" Or as the pragmatist philosopher Richard Rorty famously put it, "Why not be cruel?" On the slaughter bench of human history, the answer is more often than not, "Go ahead and be cruel if you can profit by it." After all, the dominant ethic of the ancient world was the ethic of strength. For warrior cultures, the only certain right was the "right of conquest," and the greatest virtue was virtuosic violence, hence Achilles, the Paganini of Greek violence. As Agamemnon said upon his triumphant return to Argos after the Trojan War, "My prize was conquest; may it never fail again."

We are still Greek enough for all of that. We admire the military and virtuosic violence (especially in Hollywood super-hero movies and Xbox "shooter" games), and we accept the idea that success through violence is often necessary—witness colonialism's ongoing exploitation of the vulnerable "in the national interest," and the destruction of nature, all done in the name of corporate capitalism's idea of flourishing: profit.

Secular Buddhism has no answer to Rorty's question that is not a tautology: "We should behave without cruelty because the world would flourish if we did." That is a prag-matist's wager, and it is clearly better (whatever that means) than a lot of other possibilities, but only if you are predis-posed to think in those terms, because it has no grounding, no roots, and, most obviously, no definition. My question is, why do secular/pragmatist moral wagers always end up looking like familiar religious morality? This has been the case since Kant's reasoned version of Christianity's Golden Rule, the Categorical Imperative: "Act only in accor-dance with that maxim through which you can will that it become a universal law." At least Kant was awake to what he was doing and acknowledged that the Imperative wasn't anchored to anything we could know through experience. It was a priori, or metaphysical. Shouldn't this make us pause before throwing away the transcendental basis of morality?

Batchelor's appeal to flourishing is an idol behind which one stands and dares all comers to offend against its noble purposes. But it cannot explain itself. It's like Marx's sar-donic aside in *Capital*, "Man's heart is a wonderful thing, especially when carried in the purse." But what does he mean by "heart"? This is not a moment in which he briefly forgot what he was about. For Marx, the idea that there is a human requirement for kindness and compassion that is more important than profit is a necessary assumption for his politic, yes, but it is also metaphysical to high heaven. He leaves the heart where he found it . . . *transcendental*. Like Marx, Simone de Beauvoir—socialist author of *When Things of the Spirit Come First* (1979)—recalled that when she became an atheist, "It felt like the world had fallen silent."[19]

Marx does not seek a transcendental origin for his critique of capitalism in part because his task was "not just to understand the world but to change it." Nonetheless, *Capital* has something of Tillich's "infinite passion" in it that led Marx to argue that humans should not be economically exploited and they shouldn't be imprisoned in a system of labor that alienates them from their humanity. For both Marx and the Buddha, the goal was liberation from what constrains us, openness to possibility, and creativity, in what Marx called "a higher form of society, a society in which the full and free development of every individual forms the ruling principle." It's our true nature.

In other words, the question isn't should we use metaphysics, because metaphysics is inevitable. We couldn't get through a day without it. The question is more like, who do you want to do your metaphysics? Corporations? New Atheists? Or should we prefer the more human metaphysics of Buddha, Marx, and Kant? One way or the other, Batchelor, too, is a metaphysician: He believes that human flourishing is the highest good, the summum bonum. The problem with Batchelor's metaphysics is that he doesn't know he's doing metaphysics, and there's nothing more dangerous than that.

The only answer to Rorty's question is situated somewhere other than where we stand in Batchelor's "everyday." I would go so far as to say that the transcendental element—whether Holy Spirit, Buddha nature, Hegel's World Spirit, or what you will—is a necessary assumption for any morality. Without it, we have only hodgepodge moralities in which "human flourishing" just happens to be one option that some people choose, and not very many at that. The idea that our primary moral concern should be with "flourishing in the everyday" is an *empty* assumption, especially empty in a world where billions of people live in emphatic want. *The* everyday *is a concept with no content.* It has, however, the unsubtle feel of the Anglo-American middle class. It is metaphysics for the comfortable. It is for those whom Marx called "capitalism's dependents." For the rest of us, the everyday is *the problem.*

It's not that Buddhism is indifferent to flourishing, but when Buddhism encourages flourishing, it does so through the idea that in order to flourish, we must move through *awareness,* especially awareness of the fact that we do not flourish in the world as it stands—in *samsara,* under capital. We flourish only when we leave that world, when we reject the causes and conditions that first formed us, the karma stream, the varied miseries of Western culture, especially the miseries that techno-capitalism, Facebook most notoriously, has dropped upon us.

We will truly flourish only when we awaken, when we take refuge in awareness, when we free ourselves from the world that we were born into, and when we change the way we live. We will flourish only when we end delusion, including the delusions of New Atheist materialists. Now that is a substantial way to understand flourishing.

Finally, why should anyone object to a secular Buddha, or a database Buddha, or a corporate Buddha, or a science Buddha? What harm do they do? Buddhism generally avoids disputes, so why contend with secularists? Maybe we should just "let go" of our concerns and get on with our private practice, perched in splendid isolation high atop Mount Zafu.

Perhaps the better question is, what form of Dharma will be available in the future for people seeking refuge from a destructive and materialist culture? Should that Dharma look like the corporate culture that surrounds it? Should it look like neuroscience? My concern with secular Buddhism is that it has the strong *tendency* to make itself complicit with social, economic, and political forces that it ought to be criticizing. Buddhism becomes an accessory to privilege and not a means of resistance for the poor, the alienated, and the exploited. It becomes like the rest of our civilization: in bondage to the law of indifference.

As Andrew Cooper and I argued in *Salon* in 2014:

> Buddhism has its own orienting perspectives, attitudes and values, as does American corporate culture. And not only are they very different from each other, they are often fundamentally opposed

to each other. Indeed, one of the foundations of Buddhism is the idea of *right livelihood*, which entails engaging in trades or occupations that cause minimal harm to other living beings. And yet in the literature of mindfulness as stress reduction for business, we've seen no suggestion that employees ought to think about—be mindful of—whether they or the company they work for practice right livelihood. Corporate mindfulness takes something that has the capacity to be oppositional, Buddhism, and redefines it. Mindfulness becomes just another aspect of "workforce preparation." Eventually, we forget that it ever had its own meaning.[20]

This sort of secularizing is really only about colonizing, or, as Indigenous scholar Jack D. Forbes has called it, *wétiko*—cultural cannibalism.[21] Imagine Batchelor saying to a Native American elder, "This business with the Great Spirit and your seances in the sweat lodge, all of that is primitive nonsense and needs to stop if you want to be a flourishing part of the modern world." To which this elder might reply, "Our ceremonies are medicine. Medicine for us and for Mother Earth and everything on her. It's the world of the Great Spirit that flourishes *while your world destroys itself*."

It's not in the *Diagnostic and Statistical Manual of Mental Disorders*, but science suffers from a narcissistic disorder that makes it fearful that something that isn't science might be true. Its fixed view is this: "Everything must look like science, must look like me. All thought must come to *my* conclusions or it will have to weather my furious disparagements." As the Buddha said, "People with fixed views roam the world offending people."[22] After secularization, what's left of Buddhism will wither, dry, and fall away, and Batchelor's *After Buddhism* will leave us exactly where we were *before* Buddhism's arrival in the West—in a world dominated by calculation.

At one time Batchelor understood the dangers for Buddhism in unbalanced assimilation to Western cultures. As he wrote in *The Awakening of the West* (1994):

> If Buddhism is to survive in the West it has to avoid the twin dangers of excessive rigidity, which will lead to marginalization and irrelevance, and excessive flexibility, which will lead to absorption by other disciplines and a loss of distinctive identity.

Simply put, whether through secularism, science, or corporate capitalism, Buddhism is being "absorbed" and is in the process of losing its identity. To use Batchelor's words against him, secularism "runs the risk of . . . losing sight of the originality, comprehensiveness and depth of the Buddha's vision in a dazzle of latter-day enthusiasms."

In spite of my criticisms of Batchelor's *After Buddhism*, the problem before us isn't of his creation. The first secularist, the man who coined the term *agnostic*, was Thomas Henry Huxley (1825–1895), also known as Darwin's bulldog. Huxley argued that religion had a place in English society, and the Bible had a place in schools, only after it had been edited by "organized common sense" so that its "shortcomings and errors" were removed. Batchelor has the same intentions for the Buddhist canon, although not even the Bulldog took to his chore with Batchelor's two-thousand-five-hundred-year meat-ax.

In the mid-nineteenth century, science's confidence in its conclusions led it to critique not only theology but also philosophy. This began with the French positivist and "social evolutionist" August Comte (1798–1857) who argued that human development had three stages: theological, metaphysical, and scientific, the scientific stage being the highest and final. Comte's positivism was followed in the early twentieth century by the logical positivism of Bertrand Russell and Ludwig Wittgenstein and the "verification principle," which contended that only direct experience and logical proof had any truth value. Logical positivism evolved into analytic philosophy, for which every meaningful statement is either logically analytic or can be confirmed by experience. Analytic philosophy is still the dominant intellectual school in Anglo-American departments of philosophy. The continental tradition of philosophy, especially German idealism and the metaphysics of Kant and Hegel, has been removed from the field, dead as the Book of Revelation.

More recently, the positivist/analytic tradition has spilled out of academia in sensational fashion in the work of the aforementioned New Atheists: Richard Dawkins (*The God Delusion*), Christopher Hitchens (*God Is Not Great*), and Steven Pinker (*How the Mind Works*) with ancillary support in the popular science works of Stephen Hawking, Richard Feynman, and Lawrence Krauss. Religion is still the main culprit, but Hawking declared that "philosophy is dead," and the purpose of the arts has been reduced to that of a "treasured heritage" (Dawkins), a treasured but useless heritage.

It is into the late years of this history that Stephen Batchelor has wandered.

III.

I would describe [The Heart Sutra] as a work of art as much as religion. And perhaps it is one more proof, if any were needed, that distinguishing these two callings is both artificial and unfortunate.

—*Red Pine*

While science has struggled to find a way to engage Buddhism that goes beyond its own proclivity to empiricism and quantification, that has not been a problem for literature and the arts. The influence of Asian culture on Western art began with the vogue of Chinoiserie in the eighteenth century and Japonisme in the late nineteenth, especially in the paintings of James McNeil Whistler. In the early twentieth century, Ezra Pound's poetry and the Imagist movement that he led were clearly indebted to the tradition of Haiku, as in his Imagist masterpiece "In a Station of the Metro":

The apparition of these faces in the crowd:
Petals on a wet, black bough.

And then there was the high-flying, freestyling bushwa of
Madame Blavatsky's Theosophical movement, from which
William Butler Yeats salvaged these intensely Mahayanist
lines: "I'm looking for the face I had/Before the world was
made." Western Buddhism's favorite poet, Rainer Maria
Rilke, was also part of the theosophist milieu, although
never a member.[23]

In the 1950s, Beat poets, writers, and jazz musi-
cians made Eastern philosophy and spirituality a public
part of their poetic practice in works like Jack Kerouac's
Dharma Bums and Allen Ginsberg's "Wichita Vortex
Sutra." Ornette Coleman, John Coltrane, Alice Coltrane,
Pharaoh Sanders, and Sun Ra brought music and spiritual-
ity emphatically together. The Beat's engagement with the
East was continued in the 1960s by the poets Gary Snyder,
W. S. Merwin, and Lawrence Ferlinghetti at City Lights
Bookstore. Anne Waldman sustains Beat Buddhism at the
Jack Kerouac School of Disembodied Poetics at Naropa
University in Boulder, Colorado, and the national poetry
community has always given her comrades. (For instance,
Philip Whalen, Michael McClure, Diane di Prima, poet
and Zen abbot Zoketsu Norman Fischer, Julie Carr, and
National Book Award winner Arthur Sze.) At present,
most contemporary poets have engaged Buddhist thought
in one way or another, whether through study and practice or through the influence of fellow poets who have
studied and practiced.

Why has poetry been so open to Eastern spirituality, Buddhism in particular? That is not an uncanny question because the answer is straightforward: They entered through the gate opened for them by Romanticism, the English poets in particular. The tradition of art making begun by the Romantics created a lineage that has endured to the present. And before the Romantics? Next to nothing. As literary critic Morse Peckham argued, Romanticism was the beginning of "history's second chapter." It was the origin of a new kind of spirituality, free of all established religions. As M. H. Abrams writes in his study of Romanticism, *The Mirror and the Lamp*:

> It was only in the early Victorian period, when all discourse was explicitly or tacitly thrown into the two exhaustive modes of imaginative and rational, expressive and assertive, that religion fell together with poetry in opposition to science, and that religion, as a consequence, was converted into poetry, and poetry into a kind of religion.

Over a century after the first Romantics, Henri Matisse designed and decorated the Christian Chapelle du Rosaire at Vence, France. But like the Romantics, Matisse insisted that any religious meaning in his creation was of his own making. "The only religion I have is my love of the work . . . I made the chapel to express myself completely, and for no other reason." Matisse was what James Joyce called "a priest of eternal imagination." Even abstract expressionism understood this; as Mark Rothko wrote, "Art to me is an anecdote of the spirit."

And in 1997, Bob Dylan affirmed Matisse and Rothko in saying, "I find the religiosity and philosophy in the music. I don't find it anywhere else. . . . I believe the songs."

This Religion of the Poets was a religion of "oceanic feeling," as the French novelist Romain Rolland called it in a 1927 letter to Sigmund Freud. Working mostly from its own Western resources, it sought to invent something that was certainly not Buddhism but that is fair to call "Buddhistic." It was on the Buddha's path without knowing it. And why shouldn't it have been? If we believe that all people possess Buddha nature, why shouldn't that nature have been looking for ways to express and develop itself in the West? Buddhism does not have a monopoly on Dharma; it may have a controlling interest, but not a monopoly.

When Buddhism proper landed definitively on our shores in the 1950s through the work of Alan Watts, D. T. Suzuki, Shunryū Suzuki, and others, there was a ready culture here that could say in recognition, like Baudelaire, "Ah, mon frère." The poets had been waiting for it for a century and a half. Some scholars, like Thānnisaro Bhikkhu, argue that in the end Romanticism was only a gate, and that Dharma alone should be our ultimate destination. But if Western art was a gate, it was a floodgate through which creation continues to flow, enriching both itself and Dharma.

∞

The Religion of the Poets was like no other in Western history. It rejected dogma; in fact, it rejected all forms of certainty and spoke instead of Spirit and the Imagination. It was a religion of wide eyes. It was deeply skeptical of any form of rationalism (William Blake's nemesis was Urizen, reason), especially since rationalism seemed to make the horrors of early industrialism possible. It opened our experience to Nietzschean "transvaluation," subverting our conventional assumptions about the world and our place in it. It tended to suggest, following Kant and German idealism, the primacy of mind in experience, Big Mind. It prized individual experience while also thinking that the individual was taken up in the All. As Ralph Waldo Emerson wrote, "No individual man was great except through the general."

Without dismissing reason, the Religion of the Poets valued the expression of intense feeling, spontaneity, intuition, and pleasure. It understood that suffering was the central human concern. It was a secular religion that *did* maintain a relation with Tillich's infinite passion. And above all it sensed that its newly discovered values would tend toward the creation of an ethical sensibility superior to that of the world as it stood. As Coleridge put it, the artist "brings the whole soul of man into activity."[24]

On our shores, it was American transcendentalism, especially Walt Whitman's *Leaves of Grass*, that not only made the poetry of the twentieth century possible, but also provided ways of thinking and trusting to a shared intuition of Big Mind that would make it possible for Buddhism to seem somehow familiar and comforting when it reached us. It was as if we were experiencing something for the second time, something we'd half-forgotten but were happy to see again. Paul Schrader suggests that the closest the West comes to

Zen unity is pantheism, but Romanticism does not see gods in nature, it sees the unity of man and nature, just as in Zen.

Romanticism even had a theory of Emptiness, the deconstructive term Buddhism uses to demystify the reified world of Ego and Things, the fixed and the dead, the habits, causes, and conditions into which we are born and which we take for reality. Romanticism didn't have a name for this practice, but one was later provided by the Russian formalist Viktor Shklovsky in his *A Theory of Prose* (1925): defamiliarization or enstrangement, in the Gerald Bruns translation. As Shklovsky explains:

> If we examine the general laws of perception, we see that as it becomes habitual, it also becomes automatic. . . . Automization eats away at things, at clothes, at furniture, at our wives, and at our fear of war. . . . And so, in order to return sensation to our limbs, in order to make us feel objects, to make a stone feel stony, man has been given the tool of art.[25]

Enstrangement is arguably the most important aesthetic concept of the nineteenth century, important in substantial part because its purpose is liberatory as well as artistic. Poetry sought to free us from habit, from what Blake called our "mind-forg'd manacles" and what Buddhism calls karma. This liberation began with four statements from Wordsworth's "Preface to the Lyrical Ballads" (1802), Coleridge's *Biographia Literaria* (1817), Shelley's "Defense of Poetry" (1822), and John Keats's letters.

Here's the earliest, in Wordsworth, his effort to resist the "savage torpor" of mind that had settled over England:

> The principal object, then, proposed in these Poems was to choose incidents and situations from common life, and to relate or describe them, throughout, as far as was possible in a selection of language really used by men, and, at the same time, to throw over them a certain coloring of imagination, whereby *ordinary things should be presented to the mind in an unusual aspect* [my emphasis].

In Coleridge the idea is expressed in this way: Poetry gives "the charm of novelty to things of every day" and awakens "the mind's attention from the lethargy of custom . . . for which, in consequence of the film of familiarity and selfish solicitude we have eyes, yet see not, ears that hear not, and hearts that neither feel nor understand."

And in Shelley: "Poetry lifts the veil from the hidden beauty of the world, and makes familiar objects be as if they were not familiar."

The poetry of John Keats enstranges by recollecting the world's original intimacy. In a letter to Benjamin Bailey, he wrote, "Nothing startles me beyond the moment . . . if a sparrow come before my window, I take part in its existence and pick about the gravel." Poetry breaks the crust of habitual expectation by abandoning the self's ordinary perspective in an act of imaginative sympathy, even if only for a sparrow. Keats called this capacity "negative capability."

It dissolves what Buddhism calls "separative consciousness." Keats is not only attentive to the sparrow as a thing with its own existential integrity; he *joins* the sparrow and through the sparrow the whole of existence.

The ethical strategy of enstrangement is to move human community from delusion (reification, the idea that things are fixed and immutable) through critique to transcendence. As Coleridge put it with lively force, "Dissolve! Diffuse! Dissipate! In order to recreate!" In other words, both Buddhism and Romanticism understand that the world as it seems is false, and we ought to make a truer and better world that is not fixed, that flows, that is kinder to others, and that seeks beauty and unity with nature.

These movements are central to Buddhist purpose. As Buddhist philosopher David Loy writes in *Lack and Transcendence* (1996):

> Buddhism does not provide a metaphysical system to account for reality but shows how to deconstruct [or enstrange] the socially conditioned metaphysical system we know as everyday reality.

What the Romantics began is the effort, continued through the Beats and beyond, to make the arts the "wisdom literature" of the West. Through art we see and know things as they really are—not fixed to a specimen board with a pin, not reified, but fluid, changing and dying beautifully moment by moment. This is the Middle Way. Neither thing nor not-thing, we live in the middle world of "as if," as the neo-Kantian philosopher Hans Vaihinger suggested in his 1911 book *The Philosophy of As If.* The late-Romantic poet Wallace Stevens called this fictional place in the middle the "necessary angel."

Buddhism and Romanticism also share the irony that awakening from the world of habit is dependent on suffering. Just as Thai forest master Ajahn Chah commented, "If suffering were such a bad thing, it wouldn't be the Buddha's first Noble Truth," so William Blake wrote, "Joy and woe are woven fine,/A clothing for the soul divine. . . ." John Keats called this irony the "vale of soul-making." The threefold reality of this vale he called the World, Intelligence, and the Human Heart. In what is perhaps the most famous of Keats's famous letters, he writes:

> That you may judge the more clearly I will put it in the most homely form possible—I will call the *world* a School instituted for the purpose of teaching little children to read—I will call the *human heart* the *hornbook* used in that school—and I will call the *child able to read*, the *Soul* made from that school and its hornbook. Do you not see how necessary a World of Pains and troubles is to school an Intelligence and make it a soul?

Keatsian Soul is "beyond good and evil." A century later, Rilke echoed Keats in the first of the *Duino Elegies*,

"We for whom grief is so often/the source of our spirit's growth—: could we exist without *them*?" And if all of this is too portentous for you, consider Dean Moriarty's conclusion in Jack Kerouac's *On the Road*, "Troubles, you see, is the generalization-word for what God exists in."

IV.

But what of transcendence? What of the beyond?

There are, of course, any number of epiphanies in the English and German Romantic canons in which the poet or artist sees beyond the assumptions of the dominant culture and stands—like the wanderer in Caspar David Friedrich's painting *The Wanderer Above the Sea of Fog*—at a pinnacle of insight. The poems of Keats's "annus mirabilis" are well-known instances, especially "Ode on a Grecian Urn" and "On First Looking into Chapman's Homer," exercises in mindful attention to the particular. These are peak moments, in "Chapman's Homer" literally so, "silent, high on a peak in Darien." Things appeared in their infinity, as William Blake wrote, "If the Doors of Perception were cleansed, every thing would appear to man as it is, infinite."

But there are more sustained examples of transcendence in poems like Wordsworth's "Ode: Intimations of Immortality from Recollections of Early Childhood" (1802–1804) that reveal a painstaking process of thinking through what is customary and what is eternal that is Nietzschean in its ambition. It's a long and intricate poem, but let's be awake to its movements, let's be mindful of its textures and see if the poem doesn't reward us for our efforts.

The traditional reading of the poem contends that it is about the dying away of Wordsworth's poetic powers. It is said to be personal and elegiac. (Never mind that at the time he was writing the poem, his powers were at their height.) But it is a more serious poem than that, I think. The poem begins with the following famous stanzas.

Stanza I

There was a time when meadow, grove, and stream,
The earth, and every common sight,
    To me did seem
    Apparelled in celestial light,
The glory and the freshness of a dream.
It is not now as it hath been of yore;--
    Turn wheresoe'er I may,
    By night or day,
The things which I have seen
I now can see no more.

Stanza II

    The Rainbow comes and goes,
    And lovely is the Rose,
    The Moon doth with delight
Look round her when the heavens are bare,
    Waters on a starry night
    Are beautiful and fair;
    The sunshine is a glorious birth;
    But yet I know, where'er I go,
That there hath past away a glory from the earth.

Contrary to what its full title might imply, the "Immortality Ode" is not a poem in praise of childhood, or the lost perfection of childhood innocence, or even of what Coleridge complained of in the *Biographia Literaria*, the idea that the child is the "best philosopher." The visions of childhood have a place in Wordsworth's thinking, but that place is subordinated to something more developed. Ultimately, Wordsworth was interested in the growth, development, and becoming of a human soul. "Ode," as Lionel Trilling long ago observed, has the narrative arc of a *bildungsroman*, a novel of spiritual growth. The poem's epigraph states this clearly: "The Child is Father of the Man."

Nevertheless, the first two stanzas have an elegiac feel in their evocation of the poet's lost capacity for vision. Where once the natural world seemed bathed in a "celestial light," these "things which I have seen I now can see no more." And, even more forcefully, "There hath passed away a glory from the earth." This is very close to Friedrich Schiller's account, in "On Naïve and Sentimental Poetry," of a permanent state of human grieving over a lost relation to nature closely associated with the loss of childhood. For Schiller, the things of nature depict "our lost childhood, something that remains ever dearest to us, and for this reason they fill us with a certain melancholy." Wordsworth articulates this feeling explicitly.

Even so, it is important to note that there is no claim in the "Ode" that this visionary capacity is something the child himself is able to understand. In fact, the child is little more than one of those things "apparelled in celestial light." As Coleridge observed comically, Wordsworth might as well have written about "a *bee*, or a *dog*, or a *field of corn*," for the child is no more conscious than they.

Stanza III

> *Now, while the birds thus sing a joyous song,*
> *And while the young lambs bound*
> *As to the tabor's sound,*
> *To me alone there came a thought of grief:*
> *A timely utterance gave that thought relief,*
> *And I again am strong . . .*

Stanza III begins as if it means to intensify this melancholy longing in "grief," but in line five it performs an about-face. "A timely utterance" provides *immediate* relief. What this mysterious utterance was, or who uttered it, or in what sense it was timely is unexplained. What is clear, though, in the suddenness of this transition is that grief and its relief are merged, are mutually dependent, as if somehow the recognition of grief *as grief* was in itself the grateful relief. The poet's mind takes its first bold step into self-recognition. The perfection of childhood is only now, in the moment of the poem, recognized as perfect, as lost, as the reason for grief *and* as grief's remedy.

Stanza IV

> *Ye blessed Creatures, I have heard the call*
> *Ye to each other make; I see*
> *The heavens laugh with you in your jubilee;*
> *My heart is at your festival,*
> *My head hath its coronal,*
> *The fulness of your bliss, I feel—I feel it all.*

. . .

> —But there's a Tree, of many, one,
> A single Field which I have looked upon,
> Both of them speak of something that is gone:
> The Pansy at my feet
> Doth the same tale repeat:
> Whither is fled the visionary gleam?
> Where is it now, the glory and the dream?

Stanza IV continues the process of discriminating the child from the poet. The poet is allowed a brief return to the joys of childhood's visionary seeing, but it is a joy tempered by his own self-awareness. Like an animal, the child does not know that it is joyful. Only the poet knows that. Which is a way of saying that the child and its world truly are "joyful" not for the last but for the *first* time because of the poet's contemplation. When the "celestial light" returns, it is not around flowers and babies; it is a "coronal" around the head of the poet himself!

Everything happens at once, in an "intimation," something like what Zen calls *kenpo*, "sudden enlightenment." Far from being a lament about the lost creative powers of childhood, the poet directly states that "I again am strong." Strangely, it seems that he's strong *because* he has moved beyond childhood's vision, and *because* he no longer lives in childhood's lack of self-awareness.

Stanza V

> Our birth is but a sleep and a forgetting:
> The Soul that rises with us, our life's Star,
> Hath had elsewhere its setting,

And cometh from afar:
Not in entire forgetfulness,
And not in utter nakedness,
But trailing clouds of glory do we come
From God, who is our home:
Heaven lies about us in our infancy!

The first half of stanza V introduces the Soul, coming from its spiritual home, or God, "trailing clouds of glory." The child does not come "naked" but is informed by what the Romantic era most often called Spirit. It comes with its own content and its own "vocation," as Fichte put it. Wordsworth's language is also curiously like the language of reincarnation, our birth is but a sleep and a forgetting and has its origin elsewhere. Curious.

Second half of Stanza V

Shades of the prison-house begin to close
    Upon the growing Boy,
But He beholds the light, and whence it flows,
    He sees it in his joy;
The Youth, who daily farther from the east
    Must travel, still is Nature's Priest,
    And by the vision splendid
    Is on his way attended;
At length the Man perceives it die away,
And fade into the light of common day.

The second half of the stanza introduces the poem's antag-onist, culture, the world of qualification and compromise. Even in his youth, the "prison-house" begins "to close/

Upon the growing Boy." This is what Schiller called "the misery of culture," or, a Buddhist might say, of karma, the world of destructive habit into which we are born. But even if his fate is to be absorbed by the "common day," he is still "Nature's Priest," he still "beholds the light," and will continue to do so, even if only as an "ember," no matter how profound his absorption into the world. Still, we have here something like Rousseau's alienation, the acknowledgment of the "inmate Man," everywhere in chains.

Stanza X

Then sing, ye Birds, sing, sing a joyous song!
    And let the young Lambs bound
    As to the tabor's sound!
We in thought will join your throng,
    Ye that pipe and ye that play,
    Ye that through your hearts to-day
    Feel the gladness of the May!
What though the radiance which was once so bright
Be now forever taken from my sight,
    Though nothing can bring back the hour
Of splendour in the grass, of glory in the flower;
    We will grieve not, rather find
    Strength in what remains behind;
    In the primal sympathy
    Which having been must ever be;
    In the soothing thoughts that spring
    Out of human suffering;
    In the faith that looks through death,
In years that bring the philosophic mind.

Moving forward to Stanza X, Wordsworth claims a triumph over the prison-house of the world. True, there will be no return to childhood's "splendour in the grass," but we will "grieve not," and for a simple reason: the Boy is a Man now, and he is *stronger*. What makes him stronger is the intellect, "We in thought will join your throng." The hero of the poem is the "philosophic mind," capable of coming out of suffering and looking through death. But this new power is no mere abstraction. The poet still "lives beneath [nature's] habitual sway."

> *I love the Brooks which down their channels fret,*
> *Even more than when I tripped lightly as they.*

All this time the boy has remained what he was, one with nature, in spite of culture's distortions, and now, as the poet, he *knows* it. The poet and the boy have become, in Friedrich Schelling's phrase, "self-coincident."[26]

And what has any of this to do with immortality? What exactly is the intimation an intimation of? There is no hint in the poem of a return to the "Imperial Palace" of childhood. There is no easy, sentimental reckoning. This is not about Wordsworth or you or me, although we are all ineluctably part thereof. The immortality, I think, is this: *nota bene*: *the spiritual movement that the poem describes is itself immortal*. This movement of the spirit is immortal because its drama is relived in every generation, although for most people it is not relived successfully. Most remain locked in karma/culture and are the living dead.

Whether happily or not, it is the movement of this drama that is immortal. There is always this drama of life, beauty, freedom, and spiritual wealth set against the life-in-death of culture, of administered life. Wordsworth's immortality is what Nietzsche called the "eternal return" because the eternal question for us is: Is life as you live it something that you could choose to live again and again into eternity? The poet says "yes" because, as both Nietzsche and the Buddha advised, he has found his true nature. But the boy—remembering his childhood and having experienced the misery of culture—must answer "no" because he cannot affirm an endless life-in-death. So, Wordsworth, Nietzsche, and the Buddha say to him, "You ought to wake up. You ought to live differently." This is Wordsworth's moral metaphysic.

My point here is that Wordsworth's great "Ode" is not sentimentalizing lost childhood, or regretting lost poetic powers, it is *thinking*. In fact, the *world itself is thinking through the poem*.[27] This is Wordsworth's optimism that it is possible to restore joy at a higher level and as a new power, a renewed nature. Coming to understand this power is our true vocation. Optimally, it leads toward what Hegel called "the world in love." This process is the West's ongoing enlightenment, its awareness of awareness, achieved through art, Nietzsche's "redeeming and healing enchantress."[28]

Wordsworth imagines that we have been led along the path of contemplation to nature's wholeness and to our own nobility. The reclaiming of an original wholeness, heightened by mature self-understanding, is something that, as Schiller explains, "eludes us, something we must struggle for and can hope to approach in *an endless progress* [my emphasis], even though we never attain it." This is the path the Religion of the Poets had been on for over a century when at last it joined with the Buddha's path. Like Buddhism, the poet's path presented three essential understandings: this world is false; when you live in this world, you suffer and are dissatisfied; but you can use your suffering in order to "become who you really are"—a Buddha, a poet, an artist, a Nietzschean free spirit, one of the awakened. These roles "model freedom," as Schiller thought.

As Rilke concluded the poem "Archaic Torso of Apollo," all the borders of the torso "burst like a star."

> *For here there is no place*
> *That does not see you. You must change your life.*[29]

Through the work of art, we not only learn to see, we learn that we are seen, we can't hide any longer in convention and habit, and we are now under a moral obligation to change.

Western poetry's attempt to create something "Buddhistic," solely out of its own resources, is similar to Jorge Luis Borges's short story "Pierre Menard: Author of the *Quixote*." In this story, Pierre Menard decides not to translate Cervantes's *Don Quixote* and not to recreate it in modern terms, but to literally bring the text up, sight unseen, as it was originally written, as if from his own bowels. His efforts are heroic but fragmentary. Much the same can be said of the West's unfinished enlightenment project. But Pierre Menard was never visited by Cervantes himself, and the West *has* been beautifully visited by Dharma. We can now see more clearly what the Romantic movement and the Religion of the Poets was attempting, utterly without guidance or encouragement from the surrounding world. And now their work—over two centuries of painting, music, and literature—helps us to understand and to feel at one with what is offered in the *sutras*, in meditation, and in the instruction of Dharma teachers. We have had early *intimations*, to use Wordsworth's word, of what the Buddha aspired to.

But the Buddha did not merely "leave for the West," reversing Bodhidharma's route. The astonishing thing that happened once we were introduced to Buddhism was that we *claimed* it for ourselves and Buddhism returned the favor in an act of really happy, historic mutuality. One is astonished that it happened at all, and I am grateful that I was alive for this Great Meeting. In Tillich's words, the Buddha "grasped" us in "the joy of creative communion." Tillich:

> The true ethical principle is the reconciliation with one's own being. It is not the acceptance of a strange command from outside, whether conventional or human or divine, but the command of our true being [or Buddha nature], from which we are estranged and in this sense separated. And in every morally positive act there is a reunion.

In any event, here I sit, over two hundred years after Wordsworth's great ode, and I have a powerful intimation of my own, that my thoughts are not my own. They are

Wordsworth's, they are Romanticism's, they are the Buddha's, and they are nature's. Nature fulfills itself in all of us, in *yoniso manasikara*, the womb of attention.

V.

Never before has the call to change our lives been more urgent. Science offers no such calls. It offers self-congratulation in the form of explanations, and palliatives to the exhausted, but nothing so radical as social transformation. That is so because science culture is to an unfortunate degree driven not by a sense of community but by ego: who gets the awards, who gets the grants, who gets the distinguished professorships. As Katalin Karikó, winner of the 2021 Breakthrough Prize in Life Sciences, commented to *The Guardian*:

> If so many people who are in a certain field would come together in a room and forget their names, their egos, their titles, and just think, they would come up with so many solutions for so many things. . . . But titles, promotions, older men, power, it all gets in the way.[30]

Science's culture of competition has even worse consequences in basic research, where the fight for publication in the best journals, or any journal, can lead to desperation and deception.[31]

At its best science is beautiful, but its beauties are very expensive. Science's beauties depend upon industrial civilization, which is a way of saying that science's beauties are dependent upon a social system that has been destroying life on Earth for more than two centuries. This destruction could not have happened without science's beauties.

And yet, we shouldn't blame science for being curious and inventive. We should be grateful that it has helped us to see the material world as both marvelous and mysterious. We should be grateful for what quantum physics has learned about the nature of nature, even unprovable hypotheses like "string theory." And, of course, we have learned gratitude for science the hard way during our never-ending pandemic: thank you for vaccines. But if the work of science can only be accomplished in the context of investment capital, whether from the state or from private industry, we have an existential dilemma. Big Pharma paid for the creation of vaccines but then ruthlessly monetized its product in even the poorest countries; corporate logic long ago concluded that if you can't be a paying consumer, you might as well die. All of which leaves us to wonder if scientific curiosity and inventiveness is the bright path to the future or the dead end of human evolution.

Narcissism and money. How can this be the "sound and fertile foundation" of Buddhism that Stephen Batchelor claims?

Shakespeareans might call this a "tragic flaw," but it looks to me more like something out of Hindu mythology: Kali Yuga, the last world age, because we've been moving toward this moment since the very beginning. It's been *sukha* (powers of creation) and *dukkha* (powers of destruction) in a primal dance of death that is quickly coming to a close.

When people say that we should find "solutions," what they mean is we should stay within the money system that is the source of the problems we are trying to solve. Unhappily, money's idea of a solution is that we should buy something, hence the salvation offered by the electric car. This ill logic creates the fatality that is merely typical of our species.

Neither Buddhism nor art can pretend to provide solutions to our ills, especially not technical solutions. They offer only understanding and refuge and the assurance that, ultimately, everything is always already fixed. That is our transcendental understanding quite apart from the world of techno-capital: *Everything is always already fixed.* Nothing can go wrong, even while we are confronted by things that are going terribly wrong. We don't have to save the planet. The planet will be okay. The cosmos will be okay. The multiverses beyond our cosmos will be okay. For Buddhists, spirit will be okay, the Original Brightness, the creative soul, even if we humans are not here to employ it. And if science is right and we are really only what Steven Pinker has called a "biologically selected neural computer," what difference does it make if we are gone? Let the stars resume what the poet Robinson Jeffers called their "old lonely immortal splendor" without us.

But that is not Buddhism's conclusion. Buddhism "thinks against" science materialism in the name not of the mind but of the heart/mind. Art and Dharma are making "right effort," and through right effort they do what needs to be done: they offer life. With John Ruskin, they demonstrate for the attentive that "the only wealth is life."

Beyond Money

∞

Gone, gone, gone beyond, way beyond, awake,
oh yeah!

—*Closing mantra from The Heart Sutra*

I. Living in a World Without Stars

I would set you free, if I knew how. But it isn't
free out here. All the animals, the plants, the
minerals, even other kinds of men, are being
broken and reassembled every day, to preserve
an elite few, who are the loudest to theorize on
freedom, but the least free of all.

—*Thomas Pynchon,* Gravity's Rainbow

There is no alternative.   —*Margaret Thatcher*

Who is Klaus Schwab and why are people saying such terrible things about him?

Klaus Schwab is the founder and current chairman of the
World Economic Forum (WEF) and author, with econo-

mist Thierry Malleret, of the enormously controversial book *COVID-19: The Great Reset* (2020). WEF sponsors an annual conference in Switzerland, popularly known as "Davos," an invitation-only event attended by industrial and governmental leaders from around the world. In the words of political scientist Samuel P. Huntington, the attendees of this forum are "Davos Men," a wealthy global elite who "have little need for national loyalty, view national boundaries as obstacles that thankfully are vanishing, and see national governments as residues from the past whose only useful function is to facilitate the elite's global operations."

Now, Huntington is a Harvard man and no rightwing conspiracy theorist, but this description is not far removed from the conclusions of a popular conspiracy fantasy that asserts—among many, many things—that the world is being taken over by global elites toiling against our interests under the banner of Schwab's Great Reset. The claims get woolier from there: the Great Reset has also let loose COVID-19 in order to create conditions that would allow them to take control of world politics and economics, replace national currencies with cryptocurrencies like Bitcoin, instate a communist dictatorship (aka the New World Order), and mandate a COVID vaccine containing a GPS tracker designed to provide universal police surveillance. In some versions of this theory, Donald Trump is the only leader keeping all this from happening.[1]

I say this is a conspiracy *fantasy* because there is nothing theoretical or even hypothetical about it. It is not waiting for the right arrangement of material reality to confirm its conjectures. But, then again, much of what we normally take for reality is largely a screen of clichés—fantasies—that have no basis in fact but that we live through more or less willingly anyway. Manifest destiny, American exceptionalism, equal opportunity, personal wealth as a measure of virtue, patriotism, nationalism . . . all dependent upon fantasies. As Eric Cheyfitz takes pains to clarify in his revealing book *The Disinformation Age* (2019), these clichés no longer require a relationship to "reality"—they are signifiers without a referent; they are "disinformation."

> [T]hey figure a history without a history constructed by the embedding of one fiction within another, each fiction staking its referentiality on the referentiality of the prior fictions that ground it.

These quotidian delusions provide a context in which right-wing conspiracy fantasies can seem plausible to some. For instance, if we can believe that the "Founding Fathers" convened with pure intent to provide "American freedom," why can't we imagine that people of impure intent are conspiring to take that freedom away? Even though none of this makes any sense at all, we are forbidden to say what's true: there is not now, nor has there ever been, pure or impure, something a sober person might choose to call "American freedom." To paraphrase Greg Palast, American freedom is the best freedom money can buy and always has been, and money is under no obligation to confess the con.

∽

Schwab is not the first business theorist to describe our cyber-economy and its likely future. In 1990 inventor Ray Kurzweil published *The Age of the Intelligent Machine*, and in 2001 there was Lycos CEO Bob Davis's book *Speed is Life*. Davis: "We live in a world where a company is measured by its ability to accelerate everything from manufacturing to marketing, from hiring to distributing." More recently, Richard Florida published *The Great Reset* in 2011 (a debt that Schwab does not acknowledge in his book), and in 2013 libertarian economist Tyler Cowen published *Average is Over: Powering America Beyond the Age of the Great Stagnation*. Cowen's book provides an account of the worker of the future, the "freestyler," the human working in tandem with Kurzweil's "intelligent machine." Cowen writes:

> If you and your skills are a complement to the computer, your wage and labor market prospects are likely to be cheery. If your skills do not complement the computer, you may want to address that mismatch.

The idea that the global cognoscenti are convinced that technology is the future of all global and regional economies comes as no surprise. What is perhaps surprising is an assumption that underlies their conviction: speed. *Velocity.* The idea that the future is coming at full speed has been common parlance among market savants for some time. They have argued that whether we like it or not, the cyber-economy of the future is "inevitable." How do they know it is inevitable? Because it is happening fast. Worse yet, not only is it coming fast, but, like the cosmos itself, it is *accelerating*, it is a force out of anyone's control.

On just two pages of Schwab's *The Great Reset* (pages 152–153), he uses words like *fast, speed, accelerate, catalyze, turbocharge, change,* and *quick* seventeen times. The use of those words is more than descriptive. Their repetition also has a subliminal function: anxiety. *Something is coming!* We're told the following story by all of these techno-gurus: The age of the intelligent machine is near; it is inevitable; if you don't prepare yourself for it, you will be left behind, you and your B.A. in European history. So, if you're lucky enough to go to college, be sure to study something in the STEM disciplines (science, technology, engineering, and math); if you don't, you may find yourself un- or underemployed. So get on it!

Schwab's and Cowen's bottom line is that whether you study computer science at university or not, you will end up working with intelligent machines. There's no escaping that. It's only a matter of whether the work will be with computers in a shiny Google programming warehouse in California, or with robots in a shiny Amazon fulfillment warehouse in Alabama. That's the shape that the "prisoner's dilemma" takes in the global economy of the present: shiny outside, unhappy inside, and millions of workers, isolated from each other by the very machines that are supposed to be their tools, and unable to make common cause.

This is the situation, for real. Whatever the conspiracy-minded might like to add to it, this is bad enough.

1. How is The Great Reset different from earlier theories about techno-capitalism?

There is no new global order, just a chaotic transition to uncertainty.

—*Jean-Pierre Lehmann*

Schwab differs from Tyler Cowen and his ilk in his insistence that global capital will soon have no choice except to reform itself if it wishes to avoid "doom." Schwab proposes that a global commitment to "environmental, social, and governance" crises (ESG) is necessary if capitalism is to avoid systemic failure. He claims that we will soon see "a new social conscience among large segments of the general population that life can be different." Schwab concludes that the neoliberal era is finished, its grand assumption that all problems can be fixed by markets has come to an end. In particular, COVID-19 has shown that "just-in-time" global supply chains are too fragile to work dependably and that the neoliberal model must be replaced by structures that respect the importance of regions, states, and cities. He writes:

> The model of globalization developed at the end of the last century, conceived and constructed by global manufacturing companies that were on the prowl for cheap labor, products, and components, has found its limits.

As a consequence, much more manufacturing will have to be done locally as a "hedge against disruption."

Schwab also contends that business will be "subject to greater government interference than in the past" in the form of "conditional bailouts, public procurement and labor market regulation." Like the New Deal of the 1930s, Schwab is proposing that corporations working for "stakeholders" rather than "shareholders" will save capitalism from itself and make possible another great compromise between business, government, and people.

> The pandemic struck at a time when many different issues, ranging from climate change activism and rising inequalities to gender diversity and #MeToo scandals, had already begun to raise awareness and heighten the criticality of stakeholder capitalism and ESG considerations in today's interdependent world.

The claim that global capital is going to discover its inner FDR just in time to avoid calamity is based upon the assumption that there is sensitivity and unsuspected virtue within Davos Men, who say, with Shakespeare's Shylock, "If you prick us, do we not bleed?" They, too, are people of feeling. Of course, this is just more mealymouthed special pleading by the ruling elite and is not so much a project for reform as it is another fantasy—the Davos Conspiracy Fantasy.

According to Schwab, the global elite is indeed conspiring at Davos, but it is conspiring in the name of justice, equality, and environmental health. In short, he argues that people like himself and the uber-wealthy organizations that flock to his Davos confab each year should be *trusted* to right not only their ship but all ships, in the name of a social conscience they have always possessed even if they haven't always succeeded in showing it. Most surprisingly, given that we're talking about Davos, Schwab suggests that "the ostentatious display of wealth will no longer be acceptable." So, no surprise if more Honda Civics and fewer Mercedes pull up to the curb at Davos.[2]

Slack-jawed incredulity is required here, but it is probably strongest not among capitalism's critics, people like me, but among the elite. The business elite enjoy Davos not for the preaching they hear from Schwab or from celebrities like Bono, Elton John, and Sharon Stone, but for the unique opportunity it provides for networking and deal making. The idea that they should give authority back to governments, reform labor relations, and put the needs of the environment before the need for profit will happen . . . in a pig's eye.

After all, why should they change in the ways Schwab says stakeholder capitalism requires? And why should anyone think that capitalism needs to be saved from itself? This is not the Great Depression. There was no Black Tuesday and no execs dropped from the fifteenth floor, worthless stock certificates fluttering behind.

On the contrary, the Dow Industrial Average soared in the early days of the pandemic and the wealthiest among us saw their riches greatly increase. According to a study by *24/7 Wall St.*, the net worth of America's 614 billionaires grew by a collective $931 billion during the first nine months of the pandemic. Big Tech execs have especially profited. For example, Twitter founder Jack Dorsey's personal wealth grew by $7.8 billion (a 298 percent increase). Obviously, things are good for the billionaire class.[3]

So the question becomes, since the pandemic has been profitable for the wealthy, why would they want to change anything? They have hated the New Deal for eighty years, and they have been buying up politicians to chip away at it, beginning with Ronald Reagan's attacks on big government and the welfare state. What makes anyone think that capitalism is going to do an about-face after the last forty years of clawing back New Deal concessions? Why would they do that willingly, especially now? That being the case, well might we wonder just how much climate change and social unrest they *will* tolerate before changing their ways? My suspicion is that they'll tolerate a lot, especially if stock markets continue to tell them that Everything's Jake! They have no motive for following Schwab and every profit motive for not following him.

Schwab writes as if he doesn't know his own people. While he spins ever-finer webs for a virtuous techno-future, his elite audience is thinking something far more primitive. They don't care about Schwab's sermonizing, and they don't care about Davos except that they're with the right people, the parties are nice, and maybe they'll get to hang out with Matt Damon. What the Davos elite knows in its gut is Old Testament: the cost of labor is a threat to profit. So, forget about helping workers, and don't worry so much about social protest. People are replaceable—send in the clones! After all, machines are cheap. They not only replace workers, but they are paid for with money earlier expropriated from workers themselves, with unpaid labor.[4]

Of course, stock markets are saying something quite different to the people who have had their lives turned upside down in the last three years, those millions whose only hope for survival is "quantitative easing," either "helicopter money" from the Fed or unending unemployment checks— perverse pastures of plenty. What they are being told is this: In order for the economy to thrive, we don't actually need you. We don't need your labor because robots and a few college kids will do ever more of the work. To which the unneeded must reply, "Yeah, but what am I supposed to *do*?" The answer to that question is becoming increasingly obvious: die. Die of COVID, die of poverty, die of an overdose, or die of despair, but as much as possible do it where you won't be seen.

Schwab is selling a familiar cliché: If the system has problems, the system can fix them. But that is not what is happening. Quite the opposite. If, on the one hand, Amazon has hired hundreds of thousands of new workers during the COVID crisis, it has also resisted demands for worker safety and union representation at its warehouses, and it has greatly increased its investments in automation. Amazon's warehouses are the ground floor of Tyler Cowen's vision of an economy run on the backs of "freestyling" worker/robots.

Freestyling sounds like fun, but the reality on the factory floor is awful: Between 2016 and 2019, injuries were 50 percent higher at warehouses with robots. *Bloomberg News* described life in an Amazon warehouse:

> Most of the labor in Amazon's largest fulfillment centers is divided into simple, repetitive tasks: receiving goods arriving in trucks, placing items into mesh shelving, or retrieving and speeding them along a conveyor belt in yellow plastic bins to be boxed and shipped. Most jobs are marketed to high-school graduates—no resume required, start as soon as next week—who spend 10-hour shifts standing at a single station, cogs in a giant machine built for speed and efficiency.[5]

Or as Marx wrote in *Capital*:

> [I]n the form of machinery, the implements of labour become automatic, things moving and working independent of the workman. They are thenceforth an industrial *perpetuum mobile,* that would go on producing forever, did it not meet with certain natural obstructions in the weak bodies and the strong will of its human attendants.

Fritz Lang's 1927 movie *Metropolis,* with its nightmare vision of mechanized humanity, has come full flower—a lustrous neodymium corpse flower.

And what is the market answer to the environmental threats that Schwab claims to be concerned with? What will Davos Man do, for example, about water insecurity caused by drought and desertification? Should the economy turn away from greenhouse gasses and the petroleum industry as Schwab suggests? No, the answer to a possible water shortage is, naturally, to financialize it, create market hedges against shortages by offering "water futures."

> Water joined gold, oil and other commodities traded on Wall Street, highlighting worries that the life-sustaining natural resource may become scarce across more of the world.
>
> Farmers, hedge funds and municipalities alike are now able to hedge against—or bet on—future water availability in California, the biggest U.S. agriculture market and world's fifth-largest economy.[6]

Thus, while Schwab and the World Economic Forum impose a vast smiley face on our world, a green-washing event like no other, they also show that they are, as Aeschylus wrote, "the slave of their own destruction."

2. Is there an alternative to techno-capitalism?

> The new task of the Nation States is to manage what is allotted to them, to protect the interests of the market's mega-enterprises and, above all, to control and police the redundant.
>
> —*John Berger*

We tend to think that the problem with the rich is simple: they are greedy. But it is more psychologically revealing to think of our plutocrats as residents in what Buddhism calls the God Realm. On the Tibetan Wheel of Life, the topmost realm is occupied by the winners, the wealthy, and the privileged for whom every benefit and pleasure is immediate, and all suffering and ugliness is elsewhere. But the God Realm is not only about greed, it is also about a certain psychology: anybody outside of the God Realm *doesn't exist* for the Gods, mostly because they can't be seen. It's not only that our contemporary Gods are cruel; it's that others don't exist for them except as data points—assessments of the public's trust in brands, surveys of consumer optimism, wage growth, unemployment rates, the savings rate, etc. The Gods never see us, never mix with us, don't know us except as flunkies, wage slaves, and the redundant, what Marx called an "industrial reserve army . . . kept in misery in order always to be at the disposal of capital." We're good for a laugh with our kooky conspiracy ideas, our community college degrees, our drug and alcohol melodramas, and our tawdry neighborhoods; otherwise, our world is terra incognita, a place of riot and malcontent, a place on the map where "there be monsters."[7]

Davos, on the other hand, is comforting. It is an annual public dramatization of the good life in the God Realm. It's a members-only event, badges color-coded so that there is no confusion about who belongs and who doesn't. CEOs and prime ministers get white badges; journalists and support staff get orange and purple badges. It's not as bad as swastikas and Stars of David, but you get the point.

∞

For modern residents of the God Realm, Schwab's pleas do not summon their better angels. His moralizing appeals are an annoyance: the Gods are being asked to recognize and give to people whose existence is little more than a rumor for them. The wealthy will not invite higher taxes on themselves to be used to fund enhanced social welfare and environmental conservation. It is more likely they will sigh in frustration and say, "Hey, it was hard work snagging all that dough. I didn't earn it in order to give it away for no good reason!"

A moment's pause as the Gods consider other lines of reasoning, then, "Okay, let's be honest. There are too many people. Everybody says so. And most of them are losers, sleeping on sidewalks. I am a compassionate person, but my money won't fix them. And, frankly, these are people we don't need anyway." More honestly put, "Let the world die so long as I survive."

This is not hyperbole or a joke in bad taste. It is a forced confession. As the pandemic revealed, the safety of workers in meatpacking plants, in the strawberry fields of California's factory farms, and in hospital wards was secondary to the maintenance of corporate power and profit. In the words of William Rivers Pitt, "Capitalism demanded the nation not shut down and the workers keep working, even in the teeth of a lethal pandemic." For Pitt, because minorities and immigrants do most of this work, capitalism's indifference to their well-being is a form of genocide.[8]

Reading *The Great Reset* is like walking on a boardwalk where the planks are unconnected and lie directly on the water. What waits below are the depths of the Real—death, poverty, and powerlessness. Death is the Real against which all conspiracy fantasies must be measured. The question I have is: Which conspiracy fantasy is the more deadly? The conspiracy fantasy that insists that international elites are plotting to enslave us? Or the Davos Conspiracy Fantasy that insists that stakeholder capitalism will bring greater equality and restore the Earth? Davos and QAnon: weasels fighting in a hole.

Or is it simpler and sadder than that? Is it what William Butler Yeats expressed in his poem "Meditations in Time of Civil War":

> *We had fed the heart on fantasies,*
> *The heart's grown brutal from the fare.*

If any real good is ever to come from Davos, it will come only when the Gods throw away their badges and come down from their alpine chalets. In Buddhist folklore, it was only when Prince Siddhartha left his father's palace and for the first time saw poverty, sickness, and death that the way was opened for his Awakening. Similarly, the capitalist class will not awaken until they come down from their twilight sanctuaries, their doomed Valhallas, and say, as the Dalai Lama says of himself, "I am no one special."

And you know that is never going to happen. The Gods are used to placing wagers, and they say, "The world may be burning, an angry mob may be at heaven's gate, but I'll take my chances up here."

3. Does that mean Margaret Thatcher was right? There is no alternative?

> [Workers] ought to inaugurate within the
> European beehive an age of a great swarming-out
> such as has never been seen before and through
> this act to protest against the machine, against
> capital . . . once outside, [they will] acquire a wild
> beautiful naturalness and be called heroism.
>
> —*Nietzsche, Daybreak*

The Great Reset is not a master plan for reform; it is just another enemy that capitalism has created in its own image and for its own convenience. Capitalists don't mind having critics and enemies, they sharpen the mind; but it doesn't like feeling threatened. It likes to be the home team playing the opposition within friendly confines. The elaborate moral edifice created by Klaus Schwab is a threat to no one. It is not a preamble to justice or freedom; it is just another "prison house of language," in Frederic Jameson's telling phrase. However chaotic it may seem, however contemptible in its reasoning, however ridiculous in its slow dance with robots, the one thing techno-capitalism takes comfort in is the certainty that there is nothing, especially no enemy, *outside* of it.

Inequality is surely a bad thing, destruction of the natural world a horror, but more devastating is to think there is nothing outside of techno-capitalism, no outside in which we can live differently. The only things outside of capital are the natural places it is destroying and will soon leave behind, what it glibly calls "sacrifice zones," like the Bakken oil fields in Montana and North Dakota, or the 55,000 square miles of Alberta, Canada, laid waste through tar sand extraction, Boreal songbirds up to their necks in the sludge. As the far-viewing novelist William T. Vollmann wrote in 1996:

> More and more, the privileged people will work in their homes and shop from their homes and access the Internet and play with their computers which will make the phosphor-dot worlds more and more real as the world outside continues to go to shit.[9]

The outside has disappeared, just as the stars, the heavens themselves, are disappearing because of light pollution. Even while camping on a butte in remote Zion National Park, the pollution from Las Vegas shadows the night skies—from a hundred-and-fifty miles away. Which is a tragic fact because it is a humbling privilege to look at the vastness of the heavens. But in the present, we can't even see the galaxy we're in, the Milky Way, never mind the billions of galaxies that load the rest of the cosmos and lead us to wonder if there are other cosmoses, multiverses, turning in their "old lonely immortal splendor," beyond our view but not beyond our imagining.

Now we see only what is boxed and immediately before us: property, or, much worse, virtual property, the Internet of Things. It's like living in a closet and never knowing there is a living room not far away where friends are gathered together, waiting for you. It's the technological version of the locked-in syndrome. This locked-in world for which there is no longer an outside is capitalism's World-According-to-Money. The empty sputtering of Klaus Schwab and the partygoers at Davos, and the yammering of all the would-be Paul Reveres in conspiracy land, they produce only the hot air that inflates capitalism's thrilling soap bubbles of status and the endless, lethal pursuit of money and things.

Fortunately, our situation has not always been so, nor must it so remain. Not long ago, the curious communities that we knew as universities were part of an outside, a refuge, a counter-life, especially for students of the arts and humanities. In the 1950s and 1960s tuition was cheap and so students felt freer to choose what they would study and what they would do with their lives. Now, though, universities are more like gateways to debtor's prison. For oligarchs, the ultimate benefit of student debt is that it is a very powerful tool for social regimentation. Should young people protest, the response is unequivocal and well understood, "This is the situation you were born into; it's not discussible, so make the best of it." This is naked coercion.

And it used to be that certain urban neighborhoods like the Haight in San Francisco, the East Village in New York, and the Left Bank in Paris provided cheap refuge for generations of students, artists, and miscellaneous dropouts, productively intermixed, well into the 1970s. And there were certain enlightened countercultural outposts like Taos, New Mexico; Nevada City, California; and Cazadero's Morning Star commune in Sonoma County. The powerful thing about these places was that you didn't have to live in them in order to feel like you were part of their scene. Poetry from City Lights Bookstore, punk music from the Mudd Club, and art from the lost generation at Les Deux Magots, all were disseminated internationally on Radio Zeitgeist.

Does the living memory of such places provide an alternative to what Antonio Negri calls life in the "social factory"? Yes, because when such places return, they will be bigger in scale, mostly because we're building on what was done in the past, although we may not be entirely aware of the fact. For instance, COVID-19 not only exposed how unequal we are, it also showed us how generous we are.

To take but one example, the phenomenal growth in recent disease-ridden years of "mutual aid" organizations shows there is a willingness to leave the society of money behind and create a society of friends living in what is, at least in part, a gift economy opposed to an economy run through the grift. If the Davos plan is to let more money return to the people who made it, why not let it help to create places where people can live outside of techno-capitalism? Or does Davos have the same fear that drove the Soviet Union to create the Iron Curtain: If we allow some to live in places outside of our social factory, they'll all want to live there.

And, of course, art will survive, music will still be with us, showing that our values do not have to be the machine's values. In spite of every unholy thing the world is, art offers self-valorization: This is the good, this is the beautiful, this is the world of spirit, all blessedly outside of capitalism's tear-soaked social contract. The work of artists has always been an invitation to the rest of us to join them in a great swarming out from Nietzsche's beehive. While the geniuses at Davos try to get complexity right, art wants what is true, on the other side of money, where the stars are.

II. The Samadhi of the Collective

People are addicted to money and sex
they amass possessions at any price
as soon as a tree stands out
sharp axes seek it out

—*Liu Tsung-Yuan, "Lament," (C.E. 806)*

An odd thing happened during the 2020 COVID-19 crisis and its attendant economic collapse: the familiar relationship between money and work disappeared. Most right-thinking Americans are more or less sure that money has intrinsic value that we possess when we earn it through work. As John Houseman said in the infamous television commercials he made in the 1980s for the investment firm Smith Barney, "They make money the old-fashioned way: they *earn* it."

But in the heels-over-head chaos of the 2020 economic shutdown, something strange happened—money blinked. It confessed something that threatened its legitimacy, something that a television commercial couldn't paper over. The federal government buried any notion of value as the result of work (the idea that so much work produces so much value). The assumption that "money" is related to "work" was seen for what it is: a delusion.

Even with new unemployment numbers surging higher

week after week, Wall Street went on a historic bull run, as if it were filling a hot air balloon, and all of it was "money for nothing" as the appropriately named band Dire Straits once sang. And then in broad daylight, in front of God and everybody, the Treasury Department and the Federal Reserve took us where no gold standard ever could. Billions upon billions, trillions of dollars fell from the sky. Most of it was for the purpose of keeping the banking system right side up, but some modest fraction was direct deposited into personal bank accounts, if you were lucky enough to have one of those.

Many people on unemployment discovered they were now making *more* money than they had been when they were actually doing something, showing up at nine, taking their place on the conveyor belt at the meatpacking plant or in the Share Spaces of the information economy. It made us wonder just what money is and how the rewards for work were now to be understood. It was plain to see: This money was Magic Money, money pulled out of an alchemist's hat. Money was the mysterium, the *materia prima*, the occult substance that turned what was base (labor) into something noble (gold). But where was its nobility now?

This new state of affairs seemed both bad and good. The bad thing was the sense of vertigo Magic Money created. Money seemed unmoored to any solid thing. If money had no dependable value, something we earned through work, what about the money gathered away in our bank accounts? Could that go dancing off magically like something sprinkled with malignant pixie dust? We looked at the numbers in our bank statement and they quivered unstably, like a hallucination, like Scrooge's worst nightmare shown to him by the Ghost of Christmas in Chapter 11. In the Dickens story, Scrooge learns to be generous with his money, but he does not learn that the stuff is unreal, a "pure semblance," as Marx called it. We began to suspect that our lives had been based upon an illusion that should have been obvious to us from the beginning. Once again, we were returned to the moment that Marx and Engels wrote of in *The Communist Manifesto*, "All that is solid melts into air." With inflation at 8% in 2022, this is a secret to no one.

The possible good in this situation was that with our normal world now standing on its head, the crisis became an opportunity to reconsider what we once thought to be solid and holy. We asked, "If Magic Money can be showered upon us this year, why not other years, why not every year? Maybe that's what socialists mean by 'minimum basic income.'" Could money change its color and become the means for assuring universal well-being where individuals are not entirely at the mercy of circumstance, at the mercy of their zip code? Could we make the greenback a blueback, blue as the sky?

The reason most members of Congress resist such notions, especially the idea of a universal basic income, is because of what it reveals about money: it is a scam, a ploy, a ruse, a confidence trick performed by people who don't care if we live or die. Well. Aren't we in on the con now? Perhaps we should take to the street with chants of "What do we want?" "Magic Money!" "When do we want it?" "Now!"

Another obvious, and obviously peculiar, spectacle of the COVID-19 pandemic was that it brought into full public view an unsuspected relationship between the disease and money. For some inscrutable reason, it felt as if the disease and money were two facets of one dark thing. That thing was death, and its facets were virus-death and money-death. The commingling of the two was no secret to the workers who had to choose between risking infection and paying the rent. It was no secret to the family of Guadalupe Olivera, a butcher at a Tyson beef-packing plant in Richland, Washington. When his daughter asked him what special precautions were in place at the plant, he replied, "There was nothing. It was business as usual." So, did he die because of a virus, or did he die because of money?[10] Was he a warrior hero, as Trump claimed? Or was it more like what John Ruskin saw when he wrote, "Labor is that quantity of our toil which we die in."[11]

There is an existential side to money-death, as when we wonder, "With the absence of work, of the dependable flow of numbers into my bank account, will I exist? I'll look in my mirror, if I still have a mirror to call my own, and the face there will be full of worried self-scrutiny. Can't buy anything, can't measure my relation to others, *won't know who I am!*"

In response to this anxiety, most of us say, "Work is in my blood. It's our way of life, and I'm proud of it. It provides me with a steady income so that I can put bread on the table for my family." We reassure ourselves with clichés. But now we can see the irony because it was never hidden: Work/money is in our blood, all right, but it is in our blood like an "invisible enemy," in Trump's phrase, that regularly kills us. Money itself is "bleeding us dry."

Money is a killer far more deadly than a biological virus. The plague driving climate change is money. Profit. Rent seeking. "Natural resource extraction," as our statesmen drily put it. Through the single-minded pursuit of profit, humanity becomes what Reg Morrison called a "plague species."[12] All the industrial toxins released on land, water, and air, all the wasted forests and wetlands, all the petrodollars poured into the same few pockets while animals of every kind wither where they stand and fall where they stood, disconsolate. Inconsolable. Cheerless. All murdered by money. As Albert Camus wrote in *The Plague*, "[The] social order around me was based on the death sentence."

According to the medical journal *The Lancet*, nine million people died of air and water pollution in 2015.[13] And on May 4, 2020, the *Proceedings of the National Academy of Sciences* predicted that by 2070 between two and three-and-a-half billion people across the globe would be trying to live in places that had become unlivable. In an interview in *The Guardian,* Michael Pollan commented:

> As terrible as the [Corona] virus is, the heat waves, droughts, fires and floods driven by an overheated planet have killed many more people. And if current trends persist, the death toll will increase exponentially through the end of the century.[14]

We die, animals die, so that money may thrive. It's a joke fit for a Marx Brothers routine:

Chico: Right now I'd do anything for money. I'd kill somebody for money. I'd kill *you* for money.

[Harpo looks dejected.]

Chico: Hahaha. Ah, no. You're my friend. I'd kill you for nothing.[15]

One of the enduring images to come out of the COVID-19 pandemic was the pitiless spectacle of super-yachts floating offshore, as far away as possible from us, the huddled masses. This shouldn't be a surprise: The rich have always self-isolated. They've always practiced social distancing. So much so that they're not quite sure the rest of us actually exist. They've seen us on TV, read about our problems in newspapers, but they are never among us. We are a rumor to them, something they've "heard about." We are not quite real, and certainly not as real as the people in the next yacht over.

The wealthy try to protect themselves against disease not by hoarding toilet paper or freeze-dried Pad Thai; they protect themselves by hoarding money. They hoard money in order to protect themselves from money. They gather money to themselves hoping for warmth, but it only provides, as we say, cold comfort. They hoard money with no idea how much is enough. They want to feel safe, but at what point does that happen? But it's not just them, because everyone is forced to think in these anxious ways. You say, "I have some money saved, so I'm good. I think it's enough. Is it enough?" Better phone your investment planner and find out.

Or you fear that one day your monthly paycheck, or

unemployment check, or annuity, will not be direct deposited. When that happens you will text, you will email, you will phone, but there's no one there, just a message on repeat, "We're sorry, but . . . we're sorry, but . . . our system is currently unavailable. Please try again." Try again? What's the point of that? And so you scream at Siri, as if she'd know. You say, "Siri, WTF?" and Siri replies, "I'm sorry, I don't understand . . . Can we get back to work now?"

Or let's say, okay, your company, or your annuity with MetLife, does send money to you regularly, and the economy is back on track, stuff is getting made, oil is trading over one hundred dollars per barrel, it's *normal*, until it gets so hot one Manhattan Sunday that the MetLife sign high up on the fifty-ninth floor drools down the side of the building. And now you know that playing it safe, investing your little nest egg in this and that golden chance for thirty, forty, fifty years, was the straightest road to hell. The economy you were so worried about is okay now, except that it's killing you.

In coming decades many more millions, perhaps billions of people will be running from the next plague or running from a "country of origin" with average summer temperatures of one-hundred-fifteen degrees and up.[16] This is what's coming: There will be population die-offs for every species, and there will be extinction for most if not all of them. The autopsy reports will state, laconically, "Death due to complications of environmental heat exposure."

But our really primal fear is that "they might take it away from me." They? The crooked bankers and politicians, the Deep State, the lawyers, the Jews, the "gubmint"? Or perhaps it's your neighbors that will take it all away with their extensive collection of guns they've been hoarding instead of money, knowing that the Law of the AK is, in the end, the more dependable law. It's Aesop's grasshopper turned Rambo, banging on the ant's door with the butt of an assault rifle. Marx called such grasshoppers the "dangerous class":

> The social scum, that passively rotting mass thrown off by the lowest layers of old society, may, here and there, be swept into the movement by a proletarian revolution; its conditions of life, however, prepare it far more for the part of a bribed tool of reactionary intrigue.

Thus, our own Trump-loving, MAGA-hat-wearing, belly-thumping, face-mask-hating, and gun-crazy countrymen.

Through all of this, money remains unmoved. Like Ozymandias, money still says, "submit," even though its head is rolling around on the ground. It can't say anything other because *it is afraid.* Afraid of what happens if we don't submit. Afraid of what happens when we refuse its work regime and begin to self-organize and self-develop in order to create our own satisfactions—just as we are doing now in many ways. We are beginning to reclaim what Marx called our "rich individuality" in a new way—through autonomy.

The COVID-19 virus pandemic has shown us many truths, the most important of which may be that those things we once took for granted, that we thought of as the very stuff of life, are now uncertain and demand the most serious attention. The disease has created vast networks of sickness in communities around the world, but how much vaster are the networks of suffering from economic distress, the deaths of friends and family, the sadness at seeing that even the lucky survivors are physically or mentally compromised after recovery and really not so lucky at all. And behind all of that is the grinding and inescapable anxiety of uncertainty. What new horror this way comes? This suffering is now part of who we are, but, just as importantly, it is part of what we *know*.

The truths we've learned are familiar to Buddhists: human transience, in particular, but also the loss of confidence in a culture that offers us only money, unfulfilling and destructive jobs, endless consumption, and the empty platitudes of patriotism. After the pandemic, there should be no solace in these things. As Rōshi Robert Aitken wrote in *The Mind of Clover,* we have learned that "the Great Leader is a hollow man, the Law of the Market cannot prove itself, and the Nation State mocks its own values." In these plague years, his words hold firm.

It is much easier now to understand what Aitken was thinking in the 1970s. But even with his teachings, we continue to feel the gravitational pull of our cultures, no matter how badly they have failed us. We continue to fear being emotionally marooned, set adrift from our community of birth. But to belong uncritically to that community is to belong to cruelties—racism, misogyny, economic inequality—taken at our mother's tit. As the seventeenth-century Japanese Zen master Bankei said:

On account of the faults of the people who raise you, someone abiding in Buddha Mind is turned into a first-rate unenlightened being. This is something I'm sure you all know from your own experience.[17]

Or as Southern novelist Shirley Ann Grau commented on her novel *The Keepers of the House*:

No person in the rural South is really an individual. He or she is a composite of himself and his past. The Southerner has been bred with so many memories that it's almost as if memory outreaches life.[18]

As Marx wrote potently in *The Eighteenth Brumaire*, "The tradition of all dead generations weighs like a nightmare upon the brains of the living."

Moving beyond the forms—the mental realms—into which we are born is difficult, for certain, but the thing to remember is that when we turn away from the conditions into which we were born—what Jacques Derrida called our "closure"—we will not be alone. We will find fellow travelers, so to speak, because they're not hard to find. They're all around us, just as Black Lives Matter discovered to its surprise in the spring of 2020 when its protests were joined by so many white and brown people of conscience.

In the face of horror, we are going to have to turn to new

ideas about community, new ideas about who we are, a process already underway. For example, Buddhist communities in the West offer what Marx called for: a new subjectivity. Buddhism has been richly welcomed on these shores in substantial part because it has offered us a refuge from the "grasping mind" of capitalist subjectivity. It has provided a rich self-understanding that does not participate in empty consumerism or reckless egotism. Buddhist ethics reveal that the self-evident "Self" of *Homo economicus*—humanity reduced to utility and profit—is in reality only the insatiable pursuit of private benefit: my land, my money, my things.

Buddhism is the creator of communities that provide an alternative to how we have lived to this point. After all, the purpose of Buddhism is not to feel better about living in the world of suffering and delusion; its purpose is to end suffering not only for the individual but for everyone. The Buddha showed his back to the privileged world of his youth when he saw that people outside of his palace lived with poverty, sickness, and death, just as we are seeing once again in the COVID-19 pandemic. Death is in the streets for us all, a fact we acknowledge through face masks, social distancing, and refrigerated mortuary trailers stacked in a Manhattan parking lot.

Once out of the palace, the Buddha began to imagine a counterworld, the Sangha, a community that lives not through grasping at things but through kindness, compassion, and generosity. This is the reason that the Sangha is one of Buddhism's Three Jewels. It is the Jewel that anticipates a time yet to come. It is not only about an awakened individual; it is about the world awake. As Thanissara Mary

Weinberg of Sacred Mountain Sangha has written:

> While [the CORONA-19 virus] is the purveyor
> of much suffering, it has given us needed time to
> contemplate fundamental and necessary changes
> we need to undertake. . . .
>
> As we transition through the extreme contrac-
> tions of an emergent world, the hope for that brighter
> future is now replaced with the injunction to *be* that
> future. We are to let die what no longer serves, here
> at the crossroad of our last chance on Earth.
>
> The shaman is one whose final message is not
> death, but of radical rebirth and renewal. We are
> on schedule, and it is time to dream big, to dream
> beautiful, and to weave a matrix of an indestruc-
> tible diamond-like womb of love for our new story
> to take flight.[19]

The "injunction to be that future" is a revolt against the
world as it stands. Such an injunction means to cultivate an
alternative world that is not dominated by the raw cunning
of money, to move from the karma stream to the Dharma
stream. For example, Zen master Shohaku Okumura Roshi
of the Sanshin Zen Community in Bloomington, Indiana,
came to Zen specifically because he did not want to be
part of the "money-making" culture that defined postwar
Japan. He was more interested in a form of self-discovery
that Buddhism has made available to the West. And so it
should be clear that Buddhism-on-these-shores is not eso-

teric; it is something very common, and very necessary. It is a turn away from the delusion, vanity, and destructiveness of money and its attendant bigotries. It is something offered to all people regardless of whether or not they think of themselves as Buddhists.

Samadhi is solidarity.

While the Dharma path may always feel to us like something we've adopted, there are native traditions that have provided similar benefits, that have, in fact, provided the context that made Buddhism seem familiar once it appeared here—art, music, and literature, especially writing about the experience of nature as in the work of Thoreau, John Muir, and Aldo Leopold. Because of these native traditions, Buddhism feels to us like something valuable that had been lost or forgotten, but that now has been returned to us. Buddhism does not ask us to become something foreign. We don't have to become Japanese or Tibetan in order to understand it. We are only asked to *become who we really are* and who we always have been.

Like Dharma, art has shown us how to "dream beautiful," even in a context burdened with suffering. Even the most despairing work of art is an expression of hope because of the enormous energy required to bring the work into being. Without a sort of "animal faith," as the philosopher George Santayana thought of it, that energy would not be available to the artist. Art shows that there are possibilities on the other side of our world-made-for-the-convenience-of-money.

Consider the world-breaking and world-making of Vincent van Gogh's still life of boots.[*] Van Gogh bought boots at flea markets and walked around in them until they were just filthy enough, just as filthy as the world. Still life was originally a decorative genre suitable for the homes of Netherland's burgers, the lowest of the pictorial genres. Van Gogh holds the still life genre up by its ankles and shakes the coins and stolen silverware out of its pockets, and then transforms it. The viewer should not look at the painting with a mind that wonders about the "subject," these less-than-ordinary boots, and then asks, "Why has he painted dirty boots?" Neither is the painting about the conventional pleasures of *trompe l'oeil*: "They look so real that I could put them on!" because no one would want to put on such boots. Nor should the painting be looked at as a sentimental object of sociological indignation in the name of the poor. Rightly viewed, the painting transcends boots, pleasure, and art itself. It is visionary mimesis.

The boots "abide in the here and now," in the Buddha's words. We should let go of the need for the boots to carry some particular meaning that can be praised or blamed. The painting acknowledges the suffering of the people who must wear such boots, but it also honors what Kant called "the sublime," the "boundlessness" of the boots. The painting is not technically masterful in a conventional sense; in fact, Van Gogh's thick impasto—like something painted with a

---

[*] See Vincent van Gogh, *Boots* (1886), oil on canvas. Van Gogh Museum, Amsterdam. Vincent van Gogh Foundation. View at: https://www.vangoghmuseum.nl/en/collection/s0011V1962

butter knife—is indifferent to technical excellence. Instead, as Martin Heidegger observed in his essay "The Origin of the Work of Art," Van Gogh's painting "sways" between the boots and their beyond, between thing and not-thing. In Baudelaire's phrase, it "lulls infinity in finitude" (*berçant notre infini sur le fini*).

Van Gogh's sense of the beyond provides powerful spiritual meaning. The disk of white and yellow on the other side of the boots, like the glowing background of the "relic radiation" that saturates the universe, participates in what the nineteenth-century English critic Walter Pater called "exquisite awareness." It is akin to what Zen folk mean by transmission of the Dharma—an intimate inward grasping of the world that comes alive when given outward form.

But Van Gogh's painting also has a very *practical* meaning. The painting doesn't leave us in a radiant beyond; it returns us with renewed interest to the world we live in. It presents us with an intimation of a world we might prefer to the one we endure. It is an epiphany, certainly, but also a vision of what we want in the here and now, the sacred restored to the lives we actually live. Van Gogh urges us to stop living for the false happiness provided by transient things, by boots so dirty they seem to be rotting before our eyes. This work of art suggests there are other worlds we might inhabit, worlds where what seemed squalid is made pure. Like Thanissara and the Buddha long before her, Van Gogh asks us to join him in renewing the world.

∽

Can the activities of these paths—whether artistic, or Buddhist, or both—fix anything about the world as it is presently administered? Probably not. Money may once again be thrashing in its death throes, but that is not to the credit of art or Dharma. Money will not die because we have killed it; it will die for the reason Marx long ago provided: it will die through its own fatal "internal contradictions." And the only contradiction that matters now, and in whatever future remains to us, is the ruin money has made of the Earth. An economic system dependent on a formula that means "wealth=destruction" is, obviously, the grossest of internal contradictions. It is a suicide machine, an extinction machine.

As virtually every progressive voice is saying these days, somehow/some way we need to live differently. But let's be honest, the only way we will ever live differently enough is when we stop living through money's logic. Fortunately, that's possible because we're already doing it in ways that are far from underground. We do live in generosity and friendship in places where we cultivate virtues both homely and deeply knowing—not only Sanghas, but in hometowns, intentional communities, communes, eco-villages, worker cooperatives, and whatever else we can invent. In the near future, the presence of such innately adversarial cultures will become essential to the survival of any form of life. They will be what Thich Naht Hahn called "communities of resistance."

Among the local projects that Thanissara and others like Joanna Macy are imagining are, as I mentioned earlier, mutual aid organizations that use local fundraising in order to meet local needs. (The Black Panthers's "survival programs"—

including a free Breakfast for Children program and health care services—were among the earliest experiments in radical localism.) In addition, there are grocery co-ops all over the country selling local products, and many CSA (Community-Supported Agriculture) groups, delivering boxes of fresh produce to neighbors. Like Buddhist Sanghas, CSAs are "building a new world in the shell of the old," as the Wobblies said. It is true that gun sales are "through the roof" now, but so are the sales of chicken coops.

There is also the growth of worker cooperatives, what Richard Wolff calls Worker Self-Directed Enterprises, in which workers function as their own board of directors. Wolff comments:

> [Co-ops] are concerned about profits and growth but also about the welfare of workers and their families, of surrounding communities where they live, of the quality of life and personal development on the job, and so on. In a word, a [co-op] that did well on many of those issues even if its profit rate was low would not be viewed or treated as a failure. From the [co-op] perspective, a capitalist enterprise that scored high on profits and growth but treated its workers and the surrounding community badly might well be judged a "failure."[20]

Such organizations will be called socialist by rightwing critics, and I hope they're right, but Buddhists will see them as something like a Zen economics, an economics that isn't centered on what "I" need but on compassion and generosity. They won't save the world, but they might provide what the Buddha called for in the *Sappurisa Sutta*: "association with people of integrity." Or let's call it what the Greek philosopher Epicurus sought: a Community of Friends gathered in a garden of their own making.[21] Stephen Batchelor advocated something similar in *The Awakening of the West*: "Could we not imagine an individuated form of the Dharma grounded in small autonomous communities of spiritual friendship?"

In short, our survival depends on flourishing local autonomy, wayward but enlightened communities enlarging their capacities within regions, all with the hope that more and more places around the country and around the world will see these communities and like what they see. Working in this way, we will be enacting what Carl Boggs calls "prefigurative" politics: creating now the "forms of social relations, decision-making, culture, and human experience that are the ultimate goal."[22] Occupy Wall Street was prefigurative, and so is the Buddhist Sangha.

The admirable thing about Occupy was that it made clear that what it wanted was not more equal integration into money, but an entirely new social order, because, like the police, capitalism cannot be reformed. It has to be displaced. The virtues we cultivate through such efforts will prepare us for life after money—assuming there is still life, no certainty these days. As the American poet Julie Carr said in a 2021 interview:

> Utopian dreams are necessary, especially when they're actually happening in the present. But as far as life-energy goes, I am only confident in my

ability to be useful on the hyper-local scale: community garden, foodbank, classroom. But I'm not going to pretend that's satisfying.[23]

Perhaps not, but it seems to be where we are, so we ought to make the most of it. As my favorite web opinionator William Rivers Pitt wrote after the death of Eric Carle, author of the children's book *The Hungry Caterpillar*:

> Simplicity: whatever can be done within reach of your arm. Eric Carle took 224 words, 22 lines and his paintbrush, and made the world better. Such a small thing, such an enormous thing, is within the grasp of each and every one of us. Take pain and become joy, take suffering and become learning, take rage and become the kind of love that makes children smile, and if we all do it in our own little way, we all get to come home.[24]

Samadhi is solidarity.

II.

Insight

❧

[Faith] does not appeal to experience,
which of all ludicrous things is the most
ludicrous, and which so far from making
a man wise rather makes him mad if he
knows nothing higher than this.

—*Kierkegaard*

California Karma: . . . ashes . . . ashes . . .

∽

In the popular imagination, the Buddhist concept of karma is about personal decisions that create good or bad consequences: the actions of an individual influence the future of that individual. We say, "Don't do that, it's bad karma." But there is also a karma of the collective, a communal karma. Karma is the forms and conditions already present in the world into which we were born.

To be born into a racist/evangelical/gun-crazy/truck-driving community makes it extremely likely that you will be to some degree a racist/evangelical/gun-crazy/truck-driving human. Similarly, being born into the moneyed, privileged world inhabited by the beautiful elite is likely to lead to the assumption that their abundant lives are just how things should be; after all, they're so beautiful, and so much smarter than the rest of us, a claim proven by the size of their bank accounts. Karma is the customs and the habits of mind we are born into, live through, and then pass on to the next generation. Karma is the bubble we live in thinking it is the ocean. An individual who lives in this bubble has what the Buddha called an "acquired self."

This way of understanding karma should be familiar to us. The Western rough equivalent to karma is "ideology," the conceptual world through which we come to know ourselves. As the French psychoanalyst Jacques Lacan thought, children come to consciousness by looking at whatever world is around them and thinking "I am that." (Notably, there is a book by Hindi master Sri Nisargadatta Maharaj titled *I Am That*.) We think, "I am this family, these friends, this work, these ambitions, these pleasures, these possessions, and, most importantly, these ideas and assumptions through which I conceive the world." But is it a good world? A bad world? That is not something that children are ready to consider, and by the time they are ready, they are usually so thoroughly inhabited by the reasoning of the world as it stands that self-reflection is no longer an option.

The karma of the collective is also close to what we more commonly call "culture." For California—home of the California dream or lifestyle—its culture has its own distinct qualities, as well as its own karmic debts. The origins of California's karma are famous, which makes it all the more frustrating that they are not a more prominent part of the climate conversation that has been thrust upon us, especially in light of the devastating wildfires that have ravaged the state over the last few years. This karma seems to me like something that "everybody already knows," or should. In spite of that, let's recall these origins once more, this time noticing how they are interrelated.

California genocide: After the conquest of California in 1846, native peoples died of disease, starvation, and massacre, or served as slaves, all tolerated by state authorities. As Buffy Sainte Marie asked in her song "My Country 'Tis of Thy People They're Dying"—her impassioned and wicked-smart sendup of Samuel Francis Smith's "My Country, 'Tis of Thee"— "Where in your history books is the tale/Of the genocide basic to this country's birth?" Sweet land of liberty, indeed.

Standard Oil: Natives gone and property rights established on European terms, the Earth was readied for plunder: yellow gold first, and then black gold, the more consequential of the two. Oil seeps were discovered all over the state, in Santa Barbara and Los Angeles counties most productively. Commercial development began in the 1850s and grew prodigiously after the invention of the internal combustion engine at the end of the nineteenth century.

Hollywood: Hollywood didn't create glamour, but it made glamour a tradable commodity by marketing "celebrity." MGM. 20th Century Fox. For men like Louis B. Mayer and William Fox, the studio system was just another way to make a profit. Artists they were not.

Southern California has been catching fire for a long time, with Santa Ana winds whipping flames through the canyons. But the frenzy of the Hollywood glamour professions brought a new kind of fire, the bonfire of the vanities. The lust for wealth and fame that Hollywood inspired provided kindling for self-immolation: the celebration of ego, greed, and indifference to others.

Fast Food and Shopping Malls: When the Buddha was asked, "What would you say pollutes the world and threatens it the most?" he replied, "The hunger to eat the world." California has been taking great mouthfuls of the world for most of the last two centuries, and yet claiming the innocence of eating a nineteen-cent burger and fries at Hamburger Handout, Culver City, 1958. Of course, there was never anything innocent about that burger because in twentieth and twenty-first-century America, the consumption of fast food has made over half of the adult population obese or morbidly obese. Fast food is a new form of violence for profit.[1]

As for shopping malls, not much needs to be said, especially since most of them are either dead or dying. Their place has been taken by something out of Star Wars: galactic fleets of delivery trucks bringing Amazon's apocalyptic cornucopia to our front doors. For California, and everywhere that the California lifestyle has penetrated, which is close to everywhere, nothing is ever enough—even everything is not enough.

Sprawl and Commuting: I grew up in San Lorenzo, California, a postwar "Vet Village" of ready-made homes, some assembly required. These houses were not so much built as delivered. San Lorenzo was at the origin of the California Method of prefab, assembly-line homebuilding. Levittown is better known, but it took its manufacturing principles from California. In the 1950s, inexpensive "cottages" sprang up all over the Bay Area, providing what folksinger Malvina Reynolds called "little boxes made of ticky-tacky." I listened to that song many times in the early 1960s on KSFO and never once thought she was singing about my home, but she was.

Along with the little boxes came an ever more expansive highway system through which workers commuted to city jobs and created something new in the world: epic traffic jams. These days, even five lanes in both directions are not enough. The more lanes that are built, the bigger the traffic jams, the larger the waste of fuel, the greater the air pollution, and the bigger the contribution of CO_2 to a rapidly warming planet. All of that petroleum-sourced energy expended one day after another over the last century has helped to drive the monstrous wildfires that now destroy not only forests but also the suburbs and gated subdivisions that still claim to be part of the California dream. In recent years we have learned that even major cities are at risk. In 2020 the fires came up to the city limits of Portland, Oregon, and in December 2021 a thousand homes and structures were incinerated in suburban Denver, a fire fueled by winds of one-hundred-ten miles per hour. Hundreds of miles up the coast on Washington's Olympic Peninsula, I breathed the smoke from the Oregon fires and so did people in Chicago. From a Buddhist perspective, California's karma has ripened, or, in the vernacular, its chickens have come home to roost.

Needless to say, this audit of California's karma is done in very broad strokes, and there are important things that I'm leaving out—like the ongoing horror of factory farming in the San Joaquin Valley, or Silicon Valley's roles in surveillance, gentrification, and mining for precious metals—but this is a good approximation of the world I was born into and took for settled reality when I was growing up, the aura of which lingers to this day. The single tenet of California karma was and remains, "If you can make money from violence, go ahead and be violent"—violence against people, violence against the Earth, and violence against the future.

The larger karmic reality, of which California's karma is a very elaborate variation, is money. Frederich Engels tells a relevant anecdote in *The Condition of the Working Class in England* (1845). He recalls remonstrating with a worthy "bourgeois" on a street corner in Manchester. Engels complained of the sordid and unhealthy conditions in which the working class lived. To which the bourgeois replied, "And yet there is a great deal of money made here; good morning, sir."

Of course, California has a lot of contrarian karma, most of it indebted to the 1960s counterculture, our most recent attempt to imagine life after money: livable (carless) streets, more centralized communities, sustainable local agriculture, food and work co-ops, alternative spiritual traditions, and political cultures that are more than techie slogans and really do "think different." But these ideals are more wish list than reality, because California is still one of the largest oil producers in the country (twelve million barrels per month), still prefers suburban over centralized living, still has massive commuter traffic issues in SoCal and the Bay Area, and, like everywhere else in the country, still prefers trucks and SUVs to hybrid and electric vehicles, and certainly prefers them to riding a bicycle—even a fancy e-bike.

In the end, "California" is just a word for the shameful and self-destructive political economy of the Western world, beginning with the Roman emperor Augustus's discovery that paying soldiers with money (a "donative") rather than with booty was a more efficient way to use violence for political and economic ends. We live in a world that money has made. Money could make and remake the world again and again, into infinity, and this is the world it would make. Every time.

California slowly fashioned its karma and then exported it to the rest of the world with astonishing profit. What the Earth is saying brusquely and unmistakably in reply to this dubious achievement is, "Reimagine what it means to be human or die." Or perhaps we should say, "Retrieve your own true nature or die." We are alienated from our true nature by ten thousand years of accumulated bad habits, bad habits that have been with us so long that we think they are our nature. We say, "It is in our nature to be violent," to which I like to respond, "If violence is our true nature, why is it so traumatic? Why does it cause damage to our brain's circuitry and why does it cause PTSD? Have you ever heard of anyone traumatized by acts of kindness?" Even so, our true nature is never far from us. Even now, we are capable of radical transcendence, of what Nietzsche called "self-over-coming." Overcoming our false self, that hardened shell, in order to be what we truly are—free spirits.

Transcendence is real. It is part of what is, just as climate change and viruses are part of what is. We will discover our true nature in one of two ways: we will either continue to live in delusion until the moment nears ruin, at which point we will stop caring about our private pleasures if for no other reason than that they will no longer be available to us. This is what the American economist John Kenneth Galbraith meant when he wrote, "Delusion will last until it is about to become fatal, at which point an onset of sanity is certain." After all of our self-indulgent ringing 'round the posies, this is our future: ashes, ashes, all fall down.

Or we can stop conspiring in our own defeat and begin to live as if others—other people and animals, the world, the cosmos—are what we are and that that matters more than our pleasures, our entertainments, our things, or the next cappuccino.

One of my favorite projects for radical transcendence, for good karma, is Sacred Mountain Sangha in Sebastopol, California, founded by the Dharma teachers Thanissara and her husband Kittisaro. Thanissara likes to tell a story about the first meeting with her teacher, the Thai master Ajahn Chah. His first words to Thanissara changed the direction of her life. He asked her, simply, "Have you had enough?" Enough chasing after experience, enough craving, or, as Aeschylus understood, enough "running after pleasure and ruining your people"?

California, my first home, have you had enough?

Boss Trump, or Capitalism Gone Wild

ᘏᘖ

Whom the gods would destroy, they make
crazy first.

—Ancient Latin adage

I.

The idea that Donald Trump is some sort of Mafia don—
or "wannabe gangster," as Robert DeNiro derisively put
it—has become one of the media's go-to tropes for our ex-
president. But I think that if Trump is related to the Italian
padrone, the father/boss, he is its final, debauched term. He
is the Godfather in an abyss five centuries in the making.

My evidence for this strange claim is Andrea Mantegna's
fresco of the Gonzaga family (1465–1474), part of a series of
frescoes in Federico Gonzaga's private rooms in his Mantua
palace, the so-called *Camera picta*, or "Painted Room," one
of the most celebrated rooms in art history.* In this room he
met with civic leaders and diplomats from the region.

* See Andrea Mantegna, *The Court of Gonzaga* (1465-74), walnut oil
  on plaster, Camera degli Sposi, Palazzo Ducale, Mantua. View at:
  https://www.wga.hu/html_m/m/mantegna/07/1sposi2.html

Gonzaga was the Marquis of Mantua, a city-state on the Lombard plains, a poor place compared to wealthy neighbors Florence, Milan, and Venice. (Mantua sits in the center of a triangle created by these three cities.) By profession Gonzaga was a *condottiere*, the leader of a mercenary army in the service of allied states. Most of Gonzaga's personal wealth and much of the prosperity of the city came from the retainers he was paid by his client city-states. These payments at times exceeded the income of the city itself.

But Gonzaga was something more than a mercenary because he had the benefit—revolutionary at the time—of a humanist education taken under Vittorino da Feltre, an enlightened teacher of ancient cultures and virtues. His pedagogy was to produce *uomo universale*, first among whom were Gonzaga and his wife, Barbara of Brandenburg. (Da Feltre is the gray-haired eminence in the black hat behind and between Gonzaga and his wife.)

Unlike most of the vicious and purely mercenary *condottiere* of the period (like Sigismondo Malatesta, the "wolf of Rimini"), Gonzaga valued literature and the arts, and strove to attract leading artists of the era to Mantua. Among them were Mantegna, the most advanced painter of the time, and Leon Battista Alberti, the first master of perspective, entrusted with building the city's churches and palaces.

But the thing that most strikes the modern viewer of this fresco is the implicit drama. Gonzaga has been interrupted by his *consigliere*, he of the hyper-hawk-like nose, who seems to have just rushed into the room, so vivid is the sense of motion given to him by Mantegna. He has brought Gonzaga a letter of unknown but serious content. His wife looks on in knowing attention while the others wait, close-mouthed, eyes averted, aware that whatever is in this letter is the business of the Marquis alone, the head of family and state.

The figures behind the Marquis and his wife are not mere portraits, but parts of the dramatic scene. What seems clear is that their silence is the silence not of obedience but of *trust*. They are trusting and *loyal*. They are loyal to Gonzaga for a very existential reason: without him or someone like him—someone clever, a soldier, but capable of subtle diplomacy—the more powerful states would suck up Mantua like oysters *pizzaiola*. The Marquis, in his turn, is committed not only to his family but to the city, to which he has brought prosperity, beautiful buildings, and, by draining the local swamps, some degree of health. (Pope Pius II: "All you could hear were the frogs.")

Just as important, the Gonzagas valued art. Mantegna was, in their eyes, "an extraordinary painter, unequaled in our time." Their assumption was that "a ruler becomes immortal by knowing how to honor great men." Taken together, the virtues of statecraft and the beauties of art and architecture, the Gonzagas sought to create what da Feltre called *Ca' Zoiosa*, the House of Joy.

Gonzaga's loyalty, generosity, and wisdom even allowed him to manage the bored and distracted courtiers on the fresco's far right side. They were useful, no doubt, but also vain in their sexy tan-and-orange tights, and likely to go frenzied if left to themselves. So they can just cool their heels until the Marquis is ready for them.

༨

This vast image is not, of course, how the Marquis was in reality (a warlord, after all). Rather, the image displays how he wanted to be *understood*. There is nothing of vainglory or narcissism in his portrait or in the depictions of his sober and patient family. Unlike most portraits of famous men of the period, Gonzaga is not here idealized, puffed up, clothed in golden threads (although his wife appears to be). Rather, he is dressed modestly in a comfortable robe. His feet are bare in their slippers. His conversation is measured. Although he is a *condottiere*, he is a man of peace first (in that era, being a man of peace was easier if you were also a warlord).

But this is not only how Gonzaga wanted to be understood; more importantly, this was how Gonzaga wanted his subjects, the citizens of Mantua, *to understand themselves*. This is the heart of what Italians still call *campanilismo*, love for the city of birth. Love for Mantua was not like the "love of country" that Americans claim (USA! USA!). For the city-states of the Italian Renaissance, love was earned through the city's virtues first, as well as through the beauties of the countryside around it, with which the city was in harmony.

Still, from our point of view, five hundred years after the fact, the scene looks sinister, as if the Marquis were conducting some nasty business in a Cosa Nostra flick. Perhaps he's saying, "This man is dead to me," and it looks very much like this *consigliere* knows what to do about such a person. He bows, steps back, and summons the goon squad to take someone for a ride.

There probably is something of the Gonzagas in the cultural DNA of the Mafia don. But that *capitan*, that boss, is the inverse of Federico Gonzaga. The Mafia don has no loyalty to city or state. The civic is for him just something to manipulate to his own advantage. Bribe a mayor who's "mobbed up." The don offers his community not protection but a protection racket. The only loyalty he is capable of is a veiled threat, *omertà*. The don's virtues are reduced to a love for his immediate family (tough love, to be sure) and an uncle or two. *La famiglia* celebrates this unity of purpose over plates of spaghetti, Chianti, and the only art that the don understands, the bathetic songs of old Naples: "Come Back to Sorrento"!

As for Trump: Loyalty? For Trump, everyone who comes near him is an a priori traitor to his wishes. He's just waiting for them to show their hand by trying to "reason with him," after which, as an astonishing number of White House staffers have learned, it's under the bus with you.[1] And trust? Fuhgeddaboudit. Art? His name in blazing golden lights on Trump Tower should satisfy all aesthetic need. Control the destructive impulses of his minions? The Stephen Millers and Rudy Giulianis of the world run amok on Sunday talk shows and then threaten civil violence. Beyond that, if there is anything beyond that, Trump goes on shining and stinking "like rotten mackerel by moonlight," as Congressman John Randolph of Roanoke wrote memorably in the early nineteenth century.[2]

You might judge from this ignoble tradition—from less than holy emperors to carnal popes, mercenary dukes, and Mafia dons—that Trump was the nadir, the zero degree of this long line of moral distortion. In the Impeachment Chamber, they said Trump was the worst person in the history of the country, none worse. And this might be true . . . *if it weren't for all the other people in the room!* The Clintons and the McConnells, people who use political connections to enhance personal business interests, congressmen who turn lobbyist and vice versa, and people who profit from a distinguished name—*Biden!*

This is Capitalism Gone Wild, unmoored to any ethical pillar. It is capitalism drunk, sated, uninhibited, and dancing on some Florida beach with its underpants around its ankles, free at last. Capitalism Gone Wild cares to know nothing beyond its own self-interested calculations. No humanist House of Joy, this. It has created a vast population of the "redundant"—the unneeded and unwanted—but its only plan for them is to put them into involuntary internal exile in places where rents are cheap. Rural Texas, say. If they can't do that, there's plenty of OxyContin to go around.

II.

This is not a world that can be fixed. Capitalism and the ignoble few who prosper from it are not going to change. As far as they're concerned, they're on course even though the destination may be extinction. For us, the question is no longer how to defeat and replace the capitalist nation state with a nation state of popular or socialist devising. The nation-state itself must disappear because in the face of imminent climate catastrophe, it is going to disappear whether we do anything or not. The question is how to refuse the nation state's killing structures now, in the hope that our uncertain future will be one that affirms life, and that can only be accomplished locally and, if we're lucky, regionally.

Mantegna himself can help us in this project because Mantegna may have painted the Gonzagas, but he was not like them. He was *different* from his patrons. Mantegna was one of the first to know, like Byron's Childe Harold, that he stood "among but not of them," the rich and powerful, the bloody-minded. Mantegna was one of the first artists to know that he could do what he wanted. His unique talents, and his patron's need for them, made him mostly immune to any form of inquisition. For the first time, an artist did not need to be loyal or worshipful, he needed to be free.

For Mantegna, these frescoes are about his delight in discoveries made possible by this new freedom. A new naturalism appears here, a new honesty in depicting the human face, a new willingness to express ambiguity rather than dogma, a "cosmic" landscape that captures the color and texture, if not the shape, of reality, and a new wonder in the spectacles of the secular world. He was the beginning of the counter-tradition of artist anarchists in their self-made worlds apart. Dürer. Michelangelo. Caravaggio. Picasso.

But mostly Mantegna was playing, playing while the Marquis frowned. Just as famous as the frescoes on the walls of the *Camera picta* is the oculus (an opening to the sky) on the ceiling*. All of the architectural details of the oculus are illusionistic, a groundbreaking feat of *trompe l'oeil*. The cherubs, or *putti,* are a tour de force of foreshortening. They look down on us as if from the lip of a well. When viewers stand directly beneath this illusion, looking up dizzily, they join in Mantegna's play. But does this play not also include a threatening note: the large potted plant perched precariously on the railing threatens the meaning of the courtly scenes below. It is a *détournement*, a highjacking of the room, denying the self-importance of the images on the walls. It is a piece of cultural subversion. Surely Mantegna enjoyed the thought of the pot crashing to the floor. The idea that it could, and it really does look like it could, provokes not consular sobriety but laughter. "You pay me," the artist says, "but you don't own me." Drunk on freedom, Mantegna anticipates the liberating social derangements of the Marx Brothers, Monty Python, and the guerrilla theater of the Yippees! throwing dollar bills from the gallery down onto the Wall Street floor.

Through art's transcendental brightness—the heavens show their truest blue, a butterfly cavorts, *putti* wag their hindquarters in the master's face—Mantegna calls to us. "Come on up," he says. "You never wanted to live with them anyway. Mr. Sourpuss the Marquis. Your problem child The Donald. You live with them at your own risk. So join me. The weather is perfect, the *putti* are crazy fun, and the view is great! Women and children first! The last balloon is leaving!"

* See Andrea Mantegna, Oculus of the Palazzo Ducale, Mantua, Italy. View at: https://www.wga.hu/html_m/m/mantegna/07/3sposi03.html

Freedom: It's Not About You

∽

Judd Apatow and Michael Bonfiglio's recent HBO documentary *George Carlin's American Dream* reminded me of two precious things. First, it reminded me that it was once possible for a being like George Carlin to exist at all, and then to thrive in the popular imagination. Seeing him perform again made me wonder, "How was he possible?" The answer to that question is simple enough because it's not as if Carlin was self-invented. At every stage of his career, early and late, he was an expression not only of the 1960s counterculture but of the countercultural imagination as an old and honored social force. For the most part, we know this force as art, following Andre Breton, Diego Rivera, and Leon Trotsky's insistence that art is "the natural ally of revolution." In their famous "Manifesto for an Independent Revolutionary Art," they write:

> To those who urge us, whether for today or for tomorrow, to consent that art should submit to a

discipline that we hold to be radically incompatible with its nature, we give a flat refusal, and we repeat our deliberate intention of standing by the formula: complete freedom for art.

In that peculiar moment that was the '60s counterculture, George Carlin was a distillation of what Monty Python called "something completely different." And yet, he became famous not because he was different, but because he was common. He was "one of us, one of us," as the sideshow performers chanted in Tod Browning's 1932 film *Freaks*. He happened because we were hungry for him, we were Frank Zappa's "hungry freaks," and we needed him.

Of course, the '60s counterculture wasn't self-invented either. It had its American roots in our founding performance artist Mark Twain. In *The Autobiography of Mark Twain*, Twain fearlessly declared:

> There are certain sweet-smelling, sugarcoated lies current in the world which all politic men have apparently tacitly conspired together to support and perpetuate. One of these is that there is such a thing in the world as independence: independence of thought, independence of opinion, independence of action...we are discreet sheep.

Twain had spectacular contemporaries on the American stage—the celebrated lecture tours of Charles Dickens and Oscar Wilde, a dandified counterculturalist if ever there was one. For Carlin, they were followed by more immediate influences like the Marx Brothers, Danny Kaye, and Lenny Bruce. So, that's how he happened. George Carlin was part of a lineage.

The second thing I was reminded of was at one time a countercultural given, settled truth if not law, to wit: "The American Dream is bullshit." This meant for Carlin and millions of others that the "pursuit of happiness" in the "land of the free," accomplished through the freedom to "pursue our own good in our own way" (John Stuart Mill) was a bad joke which more truly meant, as Nietzsche would have said, "You are a herd and you are being led to slaughter."

Carlin was the dark bard of American unfreedom.

The primary form that American unfreedom takes is, like Edgar Allen Poe's purloined letter, hidden in plain sight. It is that thing so common that it disappears into what we take to be the state of nature: money. The prison house of money. Appalled by the centrality of money in European culture, the Huron chief Kondiaronk said in 1703:

> I affirm that what you call money is the devil of devils, the tyrant of the French, the source of all evils, the bane of souls and slaughterhouse of the living. To imagine one can live in the country of money and preserve one's soul is like imagining one could preserve one's life at the bottom of a lake.

Recently, the prison house of money has become vividly clear for college students. Whether at university, college, or online vocational schools like Trump University, the young have had to contend with three raw facts which form a penal confine. If you want a job, you will have to go to college; if you go to college, you will have to take on debt; and if you want to pay off your debt, you will have to study what money wants you to study (for the most part, business and the STEM disciplines). In case you miss the point here, and almost everyone does, this is naked social coercion. The only thing that might need to be added is the spectacle of homelessness, so join a not-so-subtle form of domestic terrorism to the coercion because the front pages of the daily newspaper make it very clear that there but for fortune you go, with a tent and a sleeping bag, or, if you're one of the lucky, a '92 Winnebago Chieftain with transmission issues. So, you'd better stay in school whatever the cost!

Through the decades of Reaganism and neo-liberal austerity, an elite determination was made that the state should no longer pay for social infrastructure like education, health care, and affordable housing. Henceforth, social goods would be privatized and then funded through personal debt. And so college tuition became a bloated user fee, like paying through the nose for a spot in a private parking lot in Manhattan, while the expense of hospitalization became the shortest route to personal bankruptcy. As the American economist Michael Hudson writes in his book *The Destiny of Civilization*, we are experiencing a rentier takeover:

> Typical American families are obliged to spend
> whatever rises in wages they receive on the cost of

housing (rents or mortgage payments), as interest, financial fees and penalties on other borrowing, and on privatized health care and education.

Even so, this monstrous situation will continue to be called "freedom of choice," however much career counselors and personal finance advisors cringe at the idea. Because it is a lie, but it is not a lie without its own rationality. There is an old saying on the Left that goes, "Capitalism knows it will have enemies, but if it must have enemies, it will create them itself and in its own image." Make no mistake, freedom is an enemy and capitalism is deeply afraid of it. So, money offers its own bullying freedom and dares all comers to contest the claim. But, unlike Carlin, mostly we don't dare, because, as Antonio Negri writes, "Money has only one face, that of the boss."

Karl Marx drew a picture of the prison house of money in *Capital*, Volume 1: M—C—M. Capital in front, profit behind, and the infinite potential of human productivity and play shackled in the middle.

In his story "The Anarchist Banker," the Portuguese novelist Fernando Pessoa described money as a "social fiction." He wrote, "I tried to see what was the first and most important of those social fictions . . . The most important, at least in our day and age, is money." But the money story is part of a much larger complex of fictions through which we have no choice but to live. Wilde called it the "slavery of custom," and Carlin spent most of his career puncturing custom's hot air balloon. For example, as videos of and testimony about the January 6 insurrection have shown, a powerful part of that complex is the stories we tell ourselves about patriotism—a patriotism with no content other than its own fury. Whether it comes from the Rioter-in-Chief, the rioters, or the House members impaneled to investigate them, uncritical love of the nation-state generates unfreedom, violence, and, too often, death, as dear Mother Russia has shown once again in Ukraine.

As the 16th-century essayist Michel de Montaigne wrote, "Custom is the most powerful master of all things."

> Little by little and stealthily, she establishes within us the footing of her authority; but having, by this mild and humble beginning, stayed and rooted it with the aid of time, she then displays a fierce and tyrannical countenance, in opposition to which we no longer have liberty even to lift up our eyes. We see her do violence constantly to the laws of nature.

The "father of Russian socialism," Alexander Herzen, made much the same argument in *Omnia Mea Mecum Porto* (1850):

> People allow the external world to overcome them, to captivate them against their will . . . Yet this terrible power wanes from the moment when in a man's soul, instead of self-sacrifice and despair, instead of fear and submission, there arises the simple question:
> "Am I really so fettered to my environment in life and death that I have no possibility of freeing

myself from it even when I have in fact lost all touch with it, when I want nothing from it and am indifferent to its bounty?"

Herzen's solution is to remove our fetters through "self-reliance," a remedy not so far from capitalism's appeal to economic individualism and the American obsession with self-determination, with "going it alone." Happily, there are other ways of looking at the problem. From a Buddhist perspective the way out of Herzen's dilemma is to awaken from the world's orthodoxies, stop perpetuating the harm of karma/culture, and then go beyond it, into an alternative social reality, the *sangha*, human community defined not by the suspect freedoms of the ego, His Majesty the Sovereign Self, but by "right understanding" and by *metta*, kindness.

In a word, Buddhism offers not just critique but counter-culture. As Insight Meditation teacher Tuere Sala explains, "In the midst of a conditioned world, we are going to go against the grain." Giving historical depth to Sala's conviction, Robert Thurman explains in *Essential Tibetan Buddhism* that in the centuries before the Chinese invasion of Tibet Buddhism displaced the war lords and created "a counter-cultural movement that endured."

The monastic organization was a kind of inversion of the military organization: a peace army rather than a war army, a self-conquest tradition rather than an other-conquest tradition, a science of inner liberation rather than a science of liberating the outer world from the possession of others.

By creating communities against the grain, Buddhism provides a demystified enlightenment. To whatever degree we can withdraw not from the world but from worldly forms and social fictions, to that degree we are enlightened. Marxist critique finds ways to think outside of the deadly platitudes that reign over us, but Buddhism offers more: a place to stand not by our self-reliant selves but with others, in community, where we discover the importance of the Bodhisattva vow, "No one is free until we are all free."

It is clear enough that George Carlin was a critic of American unfreedom, but what's not as clear is that he, too, had made a vow to lead us to our essential freedom. This goes a long way toward explaining why his audience wrote to him not mainly with congratulations for a funny act but with gratitude. The task he set himself was difficult: how to offer freedom by performing it, on stage, in the context of that vulgar thing a standup comedy routine. Carlin said some funny things, he said some stupid things, and he said a lot of true things, but in the end it was the totality of the performance, the enactment of freedom, that mattered. Carlin understood that "art models freedom," in Friedrich Schiller's revealing phrase.

George Carlin's American Dream is shocking now not because it is saying something new. What is shocking to us is the realization that we had forgotten lifegiving things that were once familiar and full of promise. Somewhere along the way, freedom had fallen into forgetfulness. Again. Carlin was devoted to reminding us of that freedom. He created his sense of it on the stage, and then invited us to join him. Because, as HBO's title implies, George Carlin had his own style of American dreaming.

Whether approached from a Marxist or Buddhist perspective, freedom from harmful social fictions is important for our shared future. But is "raising consciousness," as we used to call it, our ultimate freedom? Late in his career Carlin seems to have discovered a freedom beyond freedom. Transcendence, perhaps, but transcendence as improvised on open mic night at the local comedy club. When Carlin was on stage, he enjoyed the freedom of a dancer, but, as Nietzsche thought, "above the dancer is the flyer and his bliss."

Consider the first five minutes of George Carlin's 1996 interview with Charlie Rose. It still drops the jaw even a quarter-century after the fact.

> I found a very liberating position for myself as an artist. And that was I sort of gave up on the human race and gave up on the American dream, and culture, and nation, and decided that I didn't care about the outcome. And that kind of gave me a lot of freedom from a distant platform to sort of watch the whole thing with a sort of wonder and pity. Not having an emotional stake in whether this experiment with humans will work.

Peering with great attention at Charlie Rose, as if he were thinking, "Dig this, Charlie. See if you can chuckle at this," he continues:

> I root for the comet, I root for the big asteroid to come and make things right. I'm rooting for that big one to come right through the hole in the

ozone layer and I want to see it on CNN . . . Philosophy asks why am I here? I know why I'm here. The show. Bring it on. We've seen comedians with some sort of political bent in their work and always implicit in the work is some kind of positive outcome. This is all gonna work. If only we can pass that bill, if we can elect him, but it's not true.

And then, turning a finger clockwise just above the table, he says, "It's circling the drain time."

And damned if Charlie Rose doesn't chuckle, as if he were thinking, "I invited a comedian on the show, so what he said must be funny," but what Carlin meant was, "Pack your shit folks, we're going away," and that wouldn't seem to be funny at all.

Not everyone was as pleased as Carlin himself seemed with this sobering turn in his career. Stephen Colbert, for one, thought that Carlin had turned nihilistic. As Colbert comments in *American Dream*, "To pursue that level of darkness in the hope that it would actually point toward something hopeful is expecting a lot from your audience, *because* all you're stating is the dark part."

But for any Buddhist watching the film, there is something oddly familiar about Carlin's new perspective. As Greg Gilman comments in a perceptive essay in *Los Angeles Magazine*, "The Zen Teachings of George Carlin," "Don't confuse awareness of the inevitable with nihilism . . . Comedy at its best is funny because it's true. The audience relates to the truth of the punchline. But truth can also hurt." Or as Carlin put it, "One of the problems of Americans is they can't really face reality. And that's why when it comes crashing down, no one is going to be prepared to handle it." The question that Carlin leaves hanging is, "Handle how?"

In Buddhism, Carlin's world of individuals who "clot" into self-destructive groups is called *samsara*, the world of suffering, dissatisfaction, and change. It is a world that can't be fixed. It is simply part of "what is," as Buddhists say, just as the murderous comets whizzing around us are a portion of what is. Comets and clotted people are aspects of what Carlin called The Big Electron, "It doesn't punish, it doesn't reward, it doesn't judge at all, it just is, and so are we, for a little while." All we can do is practice honesty and hope that through honesty we can find acceptance of what is and...laughter? Because there is something important in laughter: the possibility of other possibilities. Through laughter Carlin turned audiences into communities. They laughed together. They left the theater open to possibility, even if that sense of freedom was gone by the time they got home. Even so, Carlin's audience had been offered a "great notion," in Ken Kesey's words, and not a bloody "great nation."

Strangely, what all this reminds me of is the recent infrared images coming to us from the James Webb Space Telescope. Those stunning images convey a reality fourteen billion years in the making. And while we find the Webb images beautiful and moving, they also show us a fundamental truth about "what is": they show that all things arise, linger, and fall away including our troubled blue world. The cosmos is on fire, but we have our own little blaze here, the bonfire of the vanities—the flammable passions—greed, anger, and delusion, especially delusion, as neither Carlin nor the Buddha ever tired of showing.

When we look at the Webb images, we are not seeing Aristotle's *primum immobile*, the fixed stars, the unmoved heavens ever available for our gazing. The universe has been expanding and accelerating at 163,000+ miles per hour for the last 14 billion years, so it is very much on the move. Eventually, this acceleration, red factor flashing, will reach a point where no light will reach us from outside the gravitational confines of our own galaxy. But even this idea is a delusion because in a mere one billion years the Earth will be just another star-baked cinder, torched by our expanding sun, and there won't be anyone here to wonder where all the stars have gone.

Is that "too dark," Stephen Colbert?

Carlin claimed that imagining the end of the world was entertaining. But perhaps it is better to think that "not caring how it turns out" is comic hyperbole for the "peace that passeth all understanding." How different is Carlin's routine from what the Hindu Swami Vivekananda wrote in *Karma Yoga* in 1893?

> There is only one way to attain that freedom which is the goal of all the noblest aspirations of mankind, and that is by giving up this little life, giving up this little universe, giving up this earth, giving up heaven, giving up the body, giving up the mind, giving up everything that is limited and conditioned.

The teachings of the Buddha and the comedy of George Carlin are founded on a common perception: "Things are not
the way they seem." Our world may seem hard, durable, and
permanent, but it is not. That truth can be alarming, especially when delivered by a wit as caustic as Carlin's, but it can
also be fucking funny, as funny as the emperor's discovery
that his new clothes are his own nakedness, his gaudy social
fictions stripped away leaving only his mortality. At its best,
a joke's punchline is secular *kensho*, sudden enlightenment, a
moment in which we briefly awaken to how things really are
and laugh. What may not be so clear is that this laughter is
a summons not only to freedom, but to spiritual liberation.

III.

Joy

❦

You do not need to leave your room.
Remain sitting at your table and listen.
Do not even listen, simply wait, be
quiet, still, and solitary. The world
will freely offer itself to you to be
unmasked, it has no choice, it will roll
in ecstasy at your feet.

—*Franz Kafka*

Wagner's Passion

∞

Ah! If only I were dead!

—*Richard Wagner*

For us, the stars are not merely the universe's profligate incinerators; for us, the stars are also story-generators. Ancient people saw patterns in the stars and filled out the patterns with myth, myth that gave their lives human context rather than the disorienting feeling of being abandoned in space. We still have a need to create patterns of meaning, but we tend to do so not with stars but with people, famous people, celebrities rather than heroes. We arrange our "stars" like constellations, but the stories they reveal—in *The National Enquirer,* or on blog sites like *Hollywood Life,* or even in the culture sections of *The New York Times* and *The Guardian*—are more puzzling than revealing. "Dateline 2020: Kim Kardashian accuses Taylor Swift of lying about Kanye West!" Or, to take a blimp-sized example, what is it exactly that we want from our obsession with all things Trumplike, his presidency-by-scandal? His misadventures are as big and as wide as the *Kathasaritsagara,* the Hindu *Ocean of Story,* but what does any of that say about who *we* are? Where is the pearl in this laughable oyster?

Among the earliest of such modern *succès de scandale* is this strange story made up of some of the most luminous humans of the nineteenth century, the first public celebrities. This story is so strange that our first reaction to it is that it is false. How could these—the smartest, most sophisticated, most creative spirits in European history—how could they have behaved so childishly, with so little self-knowledge, so little kindness, and so much cruelty?

This story starts with the great German conductor Hans von Bülow. When he died in 1894, there was a celebration of his life in music. I suppose it was good to celebrate that part of his life, but the rest of it was another matter.

Von Bülow invented the modern idea of the conductor as virtuoso interpreter, as counterpart, even collaborator, to the artist/composer. He created the path that Mahler, Bruno Walter, Toscanini, and George Solti would follow. Von Bülow was not a mechanical interpreter of the score. Like Mahler, he held in contempt those who believe that the notes on the page do all the work. Incapable of thinking independently or of simply paying attention to what was really to be found in the score, they festooned the music with stupidities because, well, it sounded okay, almost right, and who could tell? (Von Bülow: "Your tone sounds like roast-beef gravy running through a sewer.")

For von Bülow and those who would follow him, the conductor's job was to remove the film of accumulated error from the score in order to feel the vitality and energy and light of the composer's creation. The first beneficiary of this new kind of conductor was Beethoven (whom von Bülow called "the New Testament of Music"). The second was Richard Wagner. He and his contemporary Franz Liszt were among the very first musicians to have a circle of admirers, propagandists, and sycophants. For Wagner, that meant *Wagnerians*. First among this School of Wagner were the symbolist poet Charles Baudelaire and the philosopher Friedrich Nietzsche. In our word, Wagner had groupies—royal groupies, artist groupies, philosopher groupies, and lots of regular groupie groupies, especially his coterie of women who seemed to find him irresistibly alluring.[1]

Beyond von Bülow's contribution to the history of orchestral music, he had a personal life in which, in odd ways, he played the part of the lazy and indifferent conductor that in a musical context he abhorred. He was *not* attentive to what he created in his relations with others, and he must have paid a terrible price for it—if he noticed. Is it possible to be horribly disappointed in life, to suffer for one's bad choices, and be oblivious to the fact? Other people did suffer for von Bülow's emotional dilettantism. Whether he noticed or cared is an open question.

Hans von Bülow married the illegitimate daughter of the virtuoso pianist Franz Liszt. Her name was Cosima. Her mother was the Countess Marie d'Agoult with whom Liszt had two illegitimate children. Cosima's marriage to von Bülow was an unhappy one, in part because von Bülow was more dedicated to father Liszt than to wife Cosima. The point is that von Bülow was imprudent (to say the least) in marrying the bastard daughter of his musical idol. What could he have been thinking? He had little human interest in her, that much was obvious from the first. Was it simply that she brought him closer to the great man?

Cosima, understandably, was bewildered and hurt by the whole thing. She resented this marriage arranged for the benefit of a father she despised. Meanwhile, old Liszt was off in his little private world where everything was what he said it was, and in which he could do what he chose to do, and receive applause and adulation for it. He was God of the Dandies. The idea that his daughter might have an objection to his self-interested shaping of the world never seemed to occur to him. I have to admit, though, that it is a very special person who can screw princesses, have children by them, and then hand off the daughters to admirers as if they were tokens of esteem.

In Cosima's case, she went along with the whole ridiculous thing because I think she didn't have a clue that there were other options, and maybe there weren't. It's also a possibility that Liszt asked von Bülow to take her off his hands because she was something that just didn't seem to have any other place. Dad was on the road with the piano, Mom was a princess and couldn't be seen too often with her children-of-indiscretion. Earlier, Liszt had dropped Cosima in this school and that, this religious institution and that, out of sight as much as possible. You know. The usual callous thing to do back then. (In another notorious example, Lord Byron stuck his illegitimate daughter in a convent, refused her heartbroken mother (sister to Shelley's wife) permission to visit, and then let the poor thing essentially rot there, alone, until she died of TB.) Making matters even more difficult for Liszt was the fact that she couldn't have been the easiest girl to find a match for; she was tall and gaunt and had a large hooking nose because of which she was called "the Stork." So, perhaps von Bülow thought he was doing her a big favor.

Meanwhile, Cosima went a little nuts.

But von Bülow's greatest musical devotion wasn't to Liszt. After hearing Liszt conduct Wagner's *Lohengrin* in its world premiere, von Bülow became a Wagnerian. He was devoted to Wagner and visited him with Cosima about the time Wagner was finishing *Tristan und Isolde*. One day while von Bülow was in rehearsal, Wagner and Cosima took a carriage ride and, just as if they were characters in Flaubert's *Madame Bovary*, did certain inappropriate little things with their fingers and lips.

But Cosima's husband wasn't the only advocate of Wagner's music. Father Liszt had also long regarded Wagner as the greatest composer in Europe. In fact, Liszt had saved Wagner from jail or worse by smuggling him out of Germany in his private carriage after the Dresden Revolution of 1849. According to legend, Wagner had fallen way out of favor with the authorities because he had burned down his own opera hall during the revolt (not good enough for him), and then paid for the production of hand grenades for the revolutionaries. Did he throw one? I don't know, but how does a person go to the trouble and expense of buying custom-made hand grenades and not throw one?

Wagner repaid all of Liszt's generosities by badmouthing and ignoring him with the connivance of Cosima, who loathed her father, the celestial *Années de pèlerinage* be damned. Cosima didn't care at all about how pretty Dad's music was, he was a shit, and she was going to get even with him for the sin of bringing her miserable self into the world. And now Wagner repaid von Bülow's kindness and support by, as Shakespeare would say, tupping his wife. "Hey, von Bülow, nice wife! Did she tell you? She blew me in the back of the carriage while we were taxied around the old town inner circle. Sweet! Now, when will you do *Tristan* in Munich?"

Believe it or not, the plot gets thicker. When Wagner and Cosima set up household in Tribschen (the house and property were gifts of barmy King Ludwig of Bavaria), they befriended the young philologist Friedrich Nietzsche. The philosopher, too, came under the powerful spell of the composer and was even, for a few years, a one-man propaganda machine for Wagner's ideas about opera, drama, Jews, and the "victory of German culture."[2] Given the perverse nature of all these relationships, it was perhaps inevitable that Nietzsche fall in love with Cosima. Because of course he did.

But, once again, Wagner repaid devotion with betrayal: during one of Nietzsche's first illnesses, Wagner sent him to his own doctor and then spread a rumor that the doctor's diagnosis confirmed Nietzsche's problem was that he was—as we might put it now, equally ungenerously—a closet queer. (Gay bashing was SOP for Wagner. As he said when his wayward disciple Karl Ritter fell out of favor, "An onanist! That says it all!") When Nietzsche heard of this betrayal, he was furious. It was then he began writing intensely hostile diatribes against the Master (*The Case of Wagner*). At the end of Nietzsche's life, his friend Franz Overbeck made an emergency trip to Turin in order to put Nietzsche in an asylum. Overbeck found him seated in a corner, singing the "gondola song," claiming to have just come from his own funeral, and reading the final proofs of *Nietzsche contra Wagner*. [3]

But the last laugh was Cosima's. She had revenge against all of these famous men. She put horns on the head of von Bülow, as noted, then she had revenge on her father. When old Liszt was dying and the world wanted to come to his side to express their thanks for his art, Cosima put the poor man in a locked room and allowed no visitors. Liszt died choking on isolation, as if Cosima had hired furniture movers to haul him out into the vacuum of space. Thus was her own childhood abandonment revenged.

For Nietzsche she had only contempt. She found him unctuous, servile, and inferior, someone good only for laughing about behind his back. She and Wagner thought of him as a useful rube (it was to Nietzsche that Wagner assigned the chore of purchasing him silken underwear or women's frillies while he was in town). Their nickname for the loyal if myopic disciple of Wagnerism was "Anselmus," after a character in *der Goldne Topf* who stumbles through life as a bumbling dreamer before finding his true vocation as an assistant scribe in a library. Cosima also goaded Wagner into conviction about Nietzsche's sexual "inversion."

As for Nietzsche's musical compositions and piano playing, they chortled about him as if he were the village idiot. They indulged his efforts to play and compose for the piano condescendingly, as if he were a pet chicken that had learned to peck out "Chopsticks." Wagner observed to the ardent philosopher that, "You play too well for a professor," tongue firmly in cheek. Von Bülow listened to Nietzsche play one of his own compositions and said to the sad crust of a man, "This may be something, but it is not music."

Even Gustav Mahler felt Cosima's wrath, in spite of the fact that, at the end of the century, he was Wagner's greatest interpreter. She refused to allow the Jew to perform on the podium at Bayreuth, even though season after season Mahler brought Wagner's operas to the stage in the musical capital of the world, Vienna, and, in his last years, in New York. Mahler was all too aware of the reason for this slight. It wasn't the first time that his Jewishness had been held against him, but he always maintained a dignified and patient silence while she acted on every vile thought.

But her greatest revenge was against Wagner himself. Wagner was a philanderer, and Cosima made him pay a heavy price for his extramarital pleasures. In fact, his last affair with the actress Carrie Pringle created such a violent quarrel that it precipitated Wagner's death: a few hours after this scene, he was found dead of a heart attack.

After his death, Cosima clutched icy fingers around the Wagner legend. She tolerated no deviance from her doctrinal instructions regarding the Master's work. Cosima censored those aspects of Wagner's life—his contempt for Christianity, his love for the pagan Greeks, etc.—that were inconvenient to the fascistic Wagner legend that she was piecing together. In her telling, Wagner was a Christian mystic, and an advocate for German nationalism and anti-Semitism. The most extreme and noxious example of her censorship was the bonfire she made of all of Nietzsche's letters to Wagner.

Forty years later, Wagner's lovingly constructed opera house in the sleepy town of Bayreuth, out in the boonies of Northern Bavaria, became a Nazi vacation resort. Hitler spent his happiest moments there, flirting with Wagner's daughter, while Himmler and S.S. dignitaries snored through *Parsifal*.

Wagner's reputation never recovered from Cosima's distortions, which is far from saying that he was an innocent. He was a charming rascal, a self-serving cad, and an anti-Semite when it served his purposes. But, ironically, he also wrote music that in its best moments expressed a spiritual love that is still compelling. Through his invention of *liebestod* (love/death) in *Tristan und Isolde,* he discovered for the West what Buddhism had long ago understood in the East: the codependency of love and death (or enlightenment and suffering); the understanding that love/death was not something happening out there among the things of the world but in the mind; and the conviction that this mind was not my mind, or your mind, but the mind's Mind. We may think of him as an unworthy vessel, but a vessel he was, a soiled angel of crazy wisdom.

Whatever the case, if we were able to ask Wagner about what was most important in his life, I think we'd hear something surprising. Wagner was often a hypocrite, but, as Samuel Johnson put it, "No man is a hypocrite in his pleasures." What Wagner would remember was how happy it made him to turn his private rooms into damask bowers brocaded and draped in the finest silks and velvets. What Wagner would remember were the silk pajamas and women's softest fineries that he wore inside his bower. What he'd remember was the feel of those dainty things against his skin, against his inner thigh. What he most loved was the plush consolation he'd feel in this bower while writing music for Tristan and his gauzy love Isolde. That was the joy that rooted in his solar plexus and soared out into the Milky Way, the River of Heaven, dispersing as smoky sfumato.

While Wagner was no hypocrite in these pleasures, still, he was mistaken. He licked the honey of his life from a razor's edge.

In all this, some people will see a magic/tragic vortex of mad energies, genius, and immortal works of art and philosophy. Wagner's life and his art together produced the kind of mythic story that the Greeks would once have translated into legends written in the night sky as constellations. "See there? That's the tip of Mahler's baton. And those three stars?

Cosima's nose." But it is a delusion to think these patterns are eternal. They are merely the irredeemable burning away of that energy we call human passion. Wagner's mighty passions were only *dukkha,* suffering, and suffering burns both brilliant and foul as methane. Our assumption is that the Wagner legend is part of art history, and that his works are timeless. But that is wrong. Nothing is timeless. Everything happens and then is gone. Just like the dying stars.

That is their beauty.

Music's Music: A Tone Poem

For David Loy

∽

La musique, c'est du bruit qui pense.

—*Victor Hugo*

"Monk's Point" is the most refined example I
have ever heard of Monk's way of bending a
piano note—not of slurring to successive notes,
but actually producing a continuous curve of
sound—an "impossible" technique.

—*Martin Williams, liner notes to* Solo Monk

When listening to music, the most wonderful thing is to
come to a moment in which we can hear the music's intelligence. In that moment, the music speaks to us both directly
and obscurely. It has many ways of doing this. For instance,
my favorite, it can speak through the *perfectly wrong note*.
Music's intelligence reveals itself in the unrolling of a scale,
or the statement of a chord establishing the music's key that
is challenged by some alien tone within it. That moment

reveals in a glancing way that the world is not what we thought it was; it reveals the world's unsuspected angularity . . . and its loveliness. Zen calls this perception *wabi-sabi*, the perfectly imperfect. It's not rounded sequences: two, four, six, eight; it's Fibonacci sequences: three, five, eight, thirteen. That is nature's idea of symmetry.

For Allen Ginsberg, this loveliness was the "apt relation of dissimilars" ("hydrogen jukebox"). Donald Barthelme expressed much the same thing as "the ugly sentence that is also somehow beautiful," or, more comically, "the creation of a strange object covered with fur which breaks your heart." The French modernist composer Olivier Messiaen was a master of the perfectly wrong. Messiaen's music *flings* wrong notes, wide of the mark, as if he were not making music but gifting the dark with stars.

Or music's intelligence comes to us in a stuttering stumble, a syncopation, in which the music suggests that it doesn't only want to move forward. That is another of Thelonius Monk's cosmic jokes. No other music syncopates as naturally as Monk's music. No other music uses "hesitation" more tellingly. It is as if the music were something Monk has sent into headlong motion only to realize that he wants to pause and say something funny to a friend. It wasn't about the notes; for him, it was about the groove, his very peculiar *groove*. As Evangelicals might say, to know music's groove is to be *justified*. To hear music's Music is to feel as if you are one of the chosen.

Monk: "The piano ain't got no wrong notes."

∽

For the philosopher Arthur Schopenhauer, music is the truest because it's the most purely expressive of the arts. Music is not imitative or representational; it has no referent. He wrote, "Music is the unconscious exercise in metaphysics in which the mind does not know that it is philosophizing." It is the inner essence of the world made directly available to the listener. Schopenhauer was the first to suggest that music has a beyond; it has its own music. As jazz bassist Victor Wooten writes, "I listened to Music in the past but only in a one-sided way. I only listened to what I wanted to hear, not what Music had to say."[1]

For Schopenhauer, music's truth is not about communication. Music does provide something, but it doesn't do that in the way that a dog might fetch the morning newspaper. Similarly, music is pleasurable, but it is not primarily about its pleasures. True, it can, as neuroscience excitedly informs us, make the dopamine flow, but that is to reduce music to a pleasure pill taken after a day at work. Neuroscience assures us that music is just part of a "flesh machine," a chemical network laid out in nerve fibers, ganglia, and synapses over which bubbling neurotransmitters flow. Any transcendental qualities in music are now to be found in a Ziploc bag with used syringes and viral swabs.

Pleasure is an aspect of what music is *for us*, but pleasure does not exhaust what music is *in itself*. What is beyond communication and beyond pleasure is . . . *music's Music*. Music's true nature reveals itself in the interval, the vibration between two notes. The *shruti* (microtones) in Indian Carnatic vocal music tirelessly searches this space-between, producing visions and intimations but never the thing itself. When Indian classical violinist L. Subrama-niam plays a raga, there is no question of the tonic note. The tonic is there. But all of the music is in the notes dancing and flying whitely around the tonic, rarely willing to light down. The tonic is only "home," always a disappointment because we didn't set off in the music only to arrive *here* again. The tonic note is only a place marker for what is unnamable.

As the modernist painter Wassily Kandinsky wrote: "The connoisseurs admire 'skill' (just as one would admire the prowess of a tight-rope dancer), and enjoy the 'painting' (as one would enjoy a pastry). Hungry souls leave as hungry as they came."[2]

I sometimes wonder why I bother to go to concerts. If it's good, if the orchestra nails the mournful sweetness of Schoenberg's *Verklartre Nacht*, even then it seems to me that in a short time there won't be much left of it, especially if some other music—the Mamas and the Papas's irresistible "Twelve Thirty," say—shuffles by. It's like a perfect tiramisu that, once the last rich forkful is gone, leaves nothing, only the vague memory of its sweetness. (Rilke: "Wait, that tastes good . . . But already it's gone.") I have little idea what tiramisu tastes like unless it is in my mouth. I only know as a kind of principle that I like it and should eat it the next time I have a chance. In a similar way, I know to return to Schoenberg because of the richness of its unfulfilled promise.

Music is the most direct way in which we experience the truth of impermanence. Music *is* impermanence. It is what Joseph Conrad called life: "The rapid blinking stumble across a flick of sunshine."

In his youth, Gustav Mahler was a music director in Kassel, Austria, a sort of edge-of-the-world musical outpost. According to his biographer, Henry-Louise de La Grange, this "stubborn young man" with his "unusual conceptions," this budding genius, had an encounter in Kassel with a young soprano. One day during a rehearsal, Mahler reproached the soprano for the "lightness of her morals." La Grange continues, "The young woman jumped up onto the piano, slapped her thighs, and advised Mahler to mind his own business, since his parched life struck her as being both grotesque and questionable." *Questionable?* Was she not suggesting that there was, as Proust would say, a hint of the "invert" in Mahler's prudery? In any event, it aided the soprano's case for continuing with her wicked ways to suggest coyly that Mahler was "one of those."

Curiously, Mahler was also criticized for the opposite, for "moving too much" when he conducted, as if he were doing the Wah-Watusi up there. Mahler indulged an otherwise congested libido through the impudence of moving while conducting. (I once saw von Karajan conduct Beethoven, and he did not "move too much." Quite Prussian he was.) From our point of view, was this nimble Viennese Jew not a horizon beyond which was . . . Elvis Presley?

As one of his own musicians wrote for an anti-Semitic newspaper:

> The Jewish Gentleman at the Vienna Opera does not conduct. It is more like the gesticulations of a dervish, and when the Kapellmeister has Saint Vitus's dance, it's really very difficult to keep time. . . . His left hand often marks the bohemian circle with convulsive jerks, scrabbles for hidden treasures, shutters and shakes, clutches, searches, smothers, battles through the waves, strangles infants, rushes, slaps; in a word it is often in a state of delirium tremens, but it does not conduct.

Strangles infants? Apparently, at that time, even bigotry had its own comic poetry.

But then there was the more masculine Mahler, the "beast of the conductor's podium." Mahler would berate his musicians in order to get the last shade of nuanced intention out of Wagner's *Die Walkure*. Some of the musicians were paralyzed with dread of Mahler and couldn't perform at all. Some responded angrily. On one infamous occasion, Mahler was threatened with a duel. To which he responded, "How can the conductor go on if he has to defend his life every time he corrects a musician?"

The musicians, on the whole, saw their service to the orchestra as a job, a way to pay rent. Few of them shared Mahler's vision of perfection. "Why should we be your idea of perfection? The audience only wants to be entertained. We amuse the people of Kassel and they go home." As Nietzsche wrote in "Wagner in Bayreuth":

> The most serious artist will try forcibly to impose seriousness on the institution of which he is part, an institution which has, however, been constructed frivolously and demands frivolity almost as a matter of principle . . .

Mahler wasn't interested in some dry notion of perfection, a mere loyalty to notes. What his musicians called perfection Mahler thought of as something like the voice of God. "Are you such brutes that you won't listen to God when He speaks to you? We are God's conduits! Without us, the people die bereft! Unconsoled!"

In the end what was left for Mahler was bitter mirth. For instance, Mahler once observed that in order to obtain the right empty and mournful sound in his Third Symphony, he needed human skulls for the percussionist to play upon. He was no doubt thinking of music critics and imagining killing them off for their otherwise useless heads.

By the end, Mahler described his experience in Kassel as "wounds to his heart," as if he had just experienced an unhappy love affair.

Mahler walked every day. He exercised vigorously until he was disabled by heart disease. Mahler was an avid cyclist as well and made some of his most important professional trips on a bicycle. Mahler was a wanderer, but he was not only wandering; he was also being pursued. He saw himself as a tragic figure, like Wagner's Siegfried, vulnerable to a spear in the back. He had a powerful sense of being the "fated-one."

As Mahler put it:

> A real terror seizes me when I see where I am heading and become aware of the road that lies ahead for music; when I understand that I have been chosen for the fearsome task. . . . Today I suddenly thought about Christ, who, on the Mount of Olives, willingly drained his cup of sorrow to the dregs.

It may be, as Schopenhauer thought, that music has no referent, and perhaps Mahler understood that, but he often seems impatient with the idea. In all of Western symphonic literature, there is no music more driven by a personal vision. His music is personally urgent, a confession, but he is also confident that his listener has felt the same torturous things—and he expresses compassion. He'd like to help. His music intends to help us. He seems impatient that he can't, perhaps, pause in the midst of the music and speak to us, tell us the truth. The truth about this world, the immediate world of suffering and delusion, and the truth about what might be beyond this suffering: "gay science," as Nietzsche thought—*joyful wisdom*. From the first, Mahler was able to see the misery of the immediate; but he was also capable of lifting his head from that misery and falling back into the infinite, like someone confident that if he did pitch himself backward, he would be caught in the arms of loved ones.

Schopenhauer's fatalism said, "Man is condemned to play the part he has undertaken to the end." But for Mahler that was only half of it. He said, "I have become what the world should become."

Conservative critics also condemned Mahler's conducting for changing the traditional way in which works were presented. Mahler did not *follow instructions*; he did not keep to precedent. What Mahler was showing the audiences of Kassel was the simple fact that what they called tradition was an accumulation of errors and laziness that had formed a dirty patina over the music, like a painting that has received one too many coats of varnish over dirt, denying the image its color, obscuring what it was supposed to protect. In essence, what Mahler said to his musicians was, "Are you asking me to proceed with a nod and a wink to the score? Why? To save you the embarrassment of acknowledging that you've been playing it wrong?"

That was Mahler's innovation—intelligence and honesty. That was why he infuriated his critics. He was an apostate to instructions. He was simply honest, always a subversive quality. And things have not changed.

There is presently no place on the face of the earth where it is safe to be honest. Most of the world's authorities think that the best place for the honest is jail or the graveyard. What our present culture says to the honest is something a little different: "No money for you." Honesty becomes synonymous with penury. That is what the young Mahler was confronted with, "No money for you unless you can stop all that shuddering and shaking up there, Herr Mahler, and provide for us the pleasures we already know."

The safe opportunity for honesty is the richest privilege. Of course, those who possess this privilege rarely use it. That's the point. They happily live in *mal foi* because, after all, it's so pleasant. As for the rest of us, its Talking Heads: "Everybody, get in line!"

The ultimate reason behind Mahler's legendary meticulousness was spiritual, not technical. Mahler felt that the spiritual truths of the great composers were socially and humanly transformative, and that if their works were allowed to become part of the hedonistic amusements of Viennese café society through the laziness of the musicians, then all that music provided was sacrilege. Like a Buddhist master, Mahler felt that everything was sacred, everything except what had been desecrated.

Mahler's diligence was a way of saying that indifference to the score was also *a failure to love.* Mahler believed, as Freud said all neurotics believe, that he could only be saved by love. (Freud provided psychoanalysis-on-the-run for Mahler in 1910 during a four-hour walk in Leiden, Netherlands, after lunch at The Gilded Turk.) But for its part, Kassel only heard, "The Jew is telling us how to love! Outrageous!"

Mahler recognized the emotional fixation on "what the Jew is doing," and displaced it through the redemptive experience of music. Astonishingly, Mahler would try to enact this redemption through the work of an anti-Semite composer, Richard Wagner. Mahler's forbearance was a most touching act of turning the other cheek.

Music has nothing to say in the absence of suffering. Music assumes suffering; it is a given. It has nothing to do without it. Even the most joyful music has suffering as an assumption—Brian Wilson's teenage symphony, *Smile*, for example, or a Mozart divertimento. Such music says, "Hey, look, in spite of everything . . . I'm happy!" When the Buddha was asked what he taught, he replied, "Suffering and the end of suffering," *dukkha* and *nirvana*. What's difficult to see in the Buddha's teaching is that the two are not different; rather, they are codependent. In music, happiness is always seen through a glass, darkly. Of course, the Austro-Hungarian Emperor Franz Joseph, Mahler's employer when he at last arrived in Vienna, didn't approve of any suffering going on in his lovely opera house. The Emperor wanted only smiles, empty-headed smiles. Like the musicians of Kassel, the Emperor assumed that people went to the opera to be entertained. So did the people themselves.

On most evenings, Mahler was really standing alone up there on the dais, not another soul in the house.

When Mahler was young, he anguished over his obscurity in Kassel, his irrelevance, but he could not change the way he worked in order to make himself more acceptable to a fallen world. In this way, he was, as Wallace Stevens thought, *noble,* a "noble rider." Mahler was subversive, but, like most artists, he wanted to subvert while being congratulated for the feat.

He was truthful, he was honest, but he too had what David Loy calls a "fame project." And eventually he would have celebrity. He became, to the Viennese on the street, "Der Mahler," the "all crushing," as they had once said of Kant.

But a contrary part of Mahler was grand enough to imagine that, whether he was in Vienna or not, his music was so comprehensive that the world would reform itself in the light of his art, and that would be acknowledgment enough. Mahler tried to make his music "model freedom" (Schiller), liberating all who heard it, bringing us closer to God. No composer ever worked harder to make us feel yearning, and to feel that we were rising up.

Mahler was confident that he could demolish Vienna's empty social forms by providing something authentic, something real, something realer than real. That's not surprising. More surprising is Mahler's temptation to think that nature itself was lacking, a lack the artifice, the artwork, could amend. As Mahler said to Bruno Walter, upon his arrival at Mahler's summer hideaway in the Hartz Mountains, "Don't bother to look at all this," meaning the forest and the mountains, "I've composed it already."[3]

Through Mahler and through Nietzsche, Romanticism changed its mind. No longer was nature the great teacher with which we were one. Nature had been found lacking and in need of supplement, and only the artist, the *Übermensch*, a being partway beyond nature, could provide that supplement. For Nietzsche, this was the "Great Noon" in which the "great man gushes forth, gushes over" and "gives birth to its god." Full of art's hubris, Mahler said, in effect, "This is what nature says, but my music is what it *wanted* to say." For Mahler, going beyond nature was the most natural thing music could do.

I have a large collection of records. To find a mint Deutsche Grammophon of David Oistrakh playing Bach and to play it on my audiophile rig and hear the deep, dark sound of the violin's wood emerging from the black depths of the vinyl is one sensual joy that I can still call mine.

But sometimes I'll look at the shelves of records and wonder just what the point is. Why so many records? I can't possibly play them all. Is my record collecting just a fetish? Why not own just one record? Perhaps what I really want is not even a record but just a note, the right note, the *Note*: the liquid distillation of all music, steely in its perfection. Then, of course, I have to wonder, "But which record holds this note?" I love each record or I wouldn't allow it a place in the dignity of The Collection. And so I must imagine that each record has the perfect note, or phrase, somewhere within it, like Buddha nature, whether it's the Stones covering Slim Harpo, Schumann's *Kinderszenen*, Miles's *In a Silent Way*, or Neutral Milk Hotel's "Oh Comely."

This happens only when music is *Music*, when it is not about making money or patronizing the suits for the major labels who provide music for "our listening pleasure." Music is Music only when it pursues its freedom and our own. This can happen even within the commercially viable, even within the Mamas and Papas's "Twelve Thirty," the "irresistible" song that I mentioned earlier. After a single meditative opening verse, the song surges suddenly forward—without a bridge, just the briefest crescendo from the drums—surges on a chorus of startling power, as if they'd just been listening to Handel's "Hallelujah Chorus": "*Young girls are coming to the ca-a-nyon!*" Okay! I don't know what that means, but let them come, those young girls! I'm all for it!

Whatever the lyrics to this song mean, the music has a meaning of its own. (Schopenhauer: "If music is too closely united to the words . . . it is striving to speak a language which is not its own.") The music announces a triumph, the possession of a capacity that we hadn't suspected was ours—it announces an *arrival*. This is "self-overcoming." We are free now to proceed in our own strength, as Nietzsche might have said (if you can hold Nietzsche and Michelle Phillips in the same thought and still function).

But these thoughts leave me looking at the perplexing mass of records and feeling a little heartbroken. This thinking is an exercise in a hopeless *longing* for something that never fully arrives and yet never feels completely defeated. I want what can't be had except in a neo-Platonic dream: everything, all the music, present all at once, the music of the spheres, art, and nature made one and reduced to a single note. For those like Mahler, the failure to achieve this dream, this heaven, was also the determination to seek it again. He was like Robert Browning in his poem "Andrea del Sarto": "A man's reach should exceed his grasp/or what's a heaven for?" And reach he did!

Music's Music is not in what it makes present, or in what it is "saying," even if what it is saying is happily subversive of commercial music written and played for people with "lazy ears," as Charles Ives liked to complain. Music's truth is in its vanishing, in its transience, in what the novelist Yukio Mishima called music's "pure continuance." Instead of supplementing a lack, as Mahler hoped to do, music makes itself both present and absent in the same instant, allowing only for the dying breath of the note's decay, the note's sad valediction. Of course, music has its rigors, its structures, its architectural theories, whether in the orthodoxy of the classical sonata or in the two-minute-thirty-second verse-verse-bridge-chorus-verse of a pop song. Even Mahler needed some sort of scaffolding, something to climb on, a crescendo to hang the Note on. This note's relationship to music is like the relationship of Mind to the activity of mind. If this note had a handle, you could lift it between your fingers and the rest of the music would dangle down like streamers.

It's like what Jack Kerouac's "holy goof" Dean Moriarty said in *On the Road*:

> "Now, man, that alto man last night had IT—he held it once he found it; I've never seen a guy who could hold so long." I wanted to know what "IT" meant. "Ah well"—Dean laughed—"now you're asking me impon-de-rables—ahem!"

Moriarty came to jazz as Saint Francis came to the almond tree. He asked the tree about God and it burst into blossom.

But the more I think about it, the more beside the point these structures, these musical scaffolds, seem. The structures are a way for us to use music to tell ourselves stories about ourselves. In short, musical structures are essentially narrative, not musical. And that's okay, of course, the telling of stories. But when it's stories told by the music industry, that's not enough. It's just the soprano slapping her thigh up on the piano.

Even worse, in its time, was the classical sonata form. Through it, His Lordship was confident in saying, "The monarchy is permanent and unyielding. It is proud and splendid." Of course, since the only audience for the sonata was the nobility itself, it also said, "We are sublime! Even the artists say so! Because we are sublime we deserve to be where we are, above and atop the mass of the *canaille*." The sonata functioned like Velázquez's court portraits: it assured the nobility of the justice and even beauty of their social elevation. This is why late Haydn, late Mozart, and just about anything Beethoven put his hand to made their patrons a little nervous. Beethoven never "got the memo."

"*Mmmyeah*, Ludwig, I heard that you put a fart in your symphony? Did you get that no fart memo?"[4]

This infamous fart was aimed directly at the sonata form and the periwigged bosses who stood upon it.

∞

The subversion of the sonata by the Romantic tone poem is also a story, a story about "strangling the last priest in the entrails of the last king," as Diderot wrote. The two musical types—sonata and tone poem—met for the first time when Duke Esterhazy burst in on Haydn in rehearsal and complained that there were "too many notes." To which an older, freer Haydn replied, "The notes are my business, your Excellency." In that moment, the Duke should have felt as if he were being assassinated, but even if he did feel this, it was too late to do anything about it: the bullet had left the gun some time ago.

Haydn announced to the Duke the end of the reign of "must." As Kandinsky might have said, Haydn gave "the eternal and immemorial answer which art gives to all questions beginning with a 'must.' There is no 'must' in art which is eternally free. From this 'must' art flees as day shuns the night."

Mahler's symphonies speak to us as world tragedies (which is, perhaps, why he wrote no chamber music—not muscular enough for the task). Mahler's music is like the Buddha's bedrock teaching, but with a caveat: "There is suffering, and there is the end of suffering . . . *if I can find it.*"

Mahler only ever wrote but one symphony. In truth, he really only ever wanted to write but one note, a drop of steely liquid, an infinitely dense black dot that, when it arrived, could be persuaded to release itself and show that it was no dot at all but an entire cosmos. Buddhism asks, "There are waves. Big waves, small waves, but where do the waves merge? In what depth?" Mahler was interested in a similar question: "There are notes, loud notes, quiet notes, but where do the notes merge?"

The dream Mahler gives us is the dream of an arduous journey to a place where we might imagine that we are home at last—no more perils and no more pain—like Odysseus in Ithaca, like Dante in paradise. This is the moment in which we discover that at last *we know what we didn't know we already knew.* This imagined moment is kin to meditative practice. We seek to leave *papancha,* conceptual proliferation, in order to find one Mind among ten thousand thoughts— or one tone among ten thousand notes.

Of course, with the natural decay of a note—the mortality to which all music is heir—the moment and its note are gone as quickly as they had come. We feel a little bereft until we realize that it is Mahler's intention to go there again. And so the climbing begins once more. Higher and higher through ascending scales that seem impossible, surely there is no octave beyond this, into the purest air. (If you could listen to the fourth movement of Mahler's Fourth Symphony now, that would be helpful.)

We could ask Mahler, "You wrote a symphony and then you wrote another symphony and another. What was wrong with the first one? Why write another?" To which Mahler might have replied, "It was insufficient to my purpose. The next one was insufficient, too, but better, so I had no choice. I had to go on, failing better with each try. I wanted to stop, but I couldn't until I got where I was going. Or until I died within the work," which he surely did in the middle of the unfinished Tenth.

As Freud might have explained to Mahler on their legendary stroll in Leiden, Mahler's desire to "arrive" was really about what any child knows, the sadness of going away and the happiness of coming back. This is the famous repetition compulsion of *fort/da*, the child's mastery of his forlorn abandonment, his anxiety about the absence of his mother, through a repeated process of throwing a ball away and having it returned by his mother. (Freud's unsurprising conclusion about Mahler's neurosis was that he had a "mother-fixation.") What Mahler seeks is an impossible return to wholeness through division. Each toss away is a sad beginning, and each happy return is tempered by the knowledge that this happiness is already gone, the loved one has walked away, and so the gesture has to be repeated, endlessly.

Mahler was like Rilke's anxious seeker after a God that doesn't recognize him, even though he has traveled so far and come so close:

> *Don't you hear my voice*
> *surging forth with all my earthly feelings?*
> *They yearn so high that they have sprouted wings*
> *And whitely fly in circles around your face.*

Mahler's music seeks *to return to a moment that it hasn't yet attained.* His music is resolute in its desire to return and to discover the ultimate articulation of music's intelligence. Mahler wants to return to that moment while *knowing* it is the moment, music's Music, the liquid distillation, the flowing steel that implies stars. He seeks to join the music without division, and not grafted stock-to-scion. Mahler wants to heal old Adam's ancient wound, his separation from God, the loved one.

But in the end, it is only disappointment that survives, because the music is, like life itself, inherently unsatisfactory. It's "only that." "A way of putting it—not very satisfactory," as T. S. Eliot wrote in "East Coker." But we at least have the consolation of knowing that we have been shown the truth, even if Mahler himself never quite saw it: fullness and lack are aspects of one thing. Mahler wrote music from a sense of lack, an obscure hurt, a neurotic "something-wrong-with-me" that he hoped music could mend. But he also saw something beyond personal hurt, something of the spirit, because in the beginning was the Note.

Or as Wagner wrote to his great love, Mathilde Wesendonck:

> Just consider my music with its delicate, oh so delicate, mysteriously flowing humors penetrating the most subtle pores of feeling to reach the very marrow of life, where it overwhelms everything that looks like sagacity and the self-interested powers of self-preservation sweeping aside all that belongs to the folly of personality and leaving only that wondrously sublime side with which we confess to our sense of powerlessness—how shall I be a wise man when it is only in such a state of raving madness that I am entirely at home.

"Subtle pores of feeling" is such a sweet touch.

The jazz musician Howard Fishman feels much like Wagner:

I was reminded of a feeling I've been fortunate enough to have known at the end of many of those long evenings on the stand. Having made myself completely available to the flow of improvised music, emboldened by the trust afforded me by my band-mates and our audience. Having followed unexplored paths, and discovered worthwhile things. Those nights walking home along the deserted streets of a dreaming city, with perhaps only a fistful of dollars in my pocket, my clothes reeking from perspiration and the stench of the club, but rich with a feeling I might call ecstatic peace.[5]

But Mahler did not really have to climb anywhere to find his Note. As a spiritual seeker, which Mahler certainly was, he did not have to go on a quest, return disappointed, and then set off again. He did not have to think like a Buddhist adept who believes that he must climb some Tibetan mountain in order to hear the last quaking word from the mouth of the last guru, only to find a note outside the guru's cave: "Out of office." Actually, Mahler arrived many times, it's why we love his music. But he was never aware that he had arrived and so felt that he had to try again. While we want to say, "Mahler, calm yourself. It's right here."

I think the Roman Catholic mystic Olivier Messiaen was aware, and for him no special note was required. Every note was the Note. A synesthetic, he wrote of color while thinking of music:

What does a rose window in a cathedral do? It teaches through image and symbol and all those figures that inhabit it—but what most catches the eye are those thousands of specks of color that ultimately resolve themselves into a single color.

In other words, again, don't mistake the music for Music. Messiaen's music is unconstrained, which frees him to use form as he likes; he uses nineteenth-century harmonics and melodic line while not being bound by them. (Just as this essay uses various literary forms (essay, story, poem, biography, criticism) without being reduced to any one of them.)

Each of the notes Messiaen's music flings out, and flings out again, is fundamental, like one quantum particle among infinitely many winking in the dark, but together creating something unitary: *Being.* For Messiaen, the Holy Ghost didn't need to be sought and found, as Mahler tried to do. Messiaen let go of the craziness of the seeking mind. *La Présence Divine* was always there, all around him, turning gracefully like the Lord of the Dance.

Living in a World that No Longer Exists: An Elegy with Bright Wings

∞

I.

There is no heavier fate than to live in a time that is not your own.

—*Vasily Grossman,* Life and Fate

Our moment is ripe with impermanence. Nearest to us, there is that form of impermanence familiar to Buddhists: birth, aging, sickness, and death. The symbolist poet Charles Baudelaire described this ordinary catastrophe in lines as forceful as Tibetan skull beads: "Time engulfs me in its steady tide/As blizzards cover corpses with their snow."[1]

But recently the ageless fear of our approaching demise has been greatly quickened by the COVID-19 pandemic. It feels as if we are now accelerating through the stages of life. If we thought we still had long, lazy years in front of us, it now feels as if many of us will be dead by the end of the week, every week, and on into the foreseeable future. Untimely deaths indeed. Anxious, we try to shut our ears to it, but we still hear what Albert Camus called "that eerie sound above, the whispering of the plague."

Of course, once we get to the other side of the COVID crisis, the catastrophe of climate change will be waiting there for us, the Sixth Great Extinction, the abrupt end of the placid Holocene and the beginning of the Anthropocene, a sure-to-be-short-lived epoch dominated by human purposes and human failures. But even that is only a part of the story because it is couched within a more fundamental extinction, the great grinding machine that is our home, Earth. Here in the Northwest, the Cascadian Subduction Zone forces the lighter North American plate up while pushing the Juan de Fuca plate down, only to see the ocean plate rise again through magma chambers, surging up volcanic conduits into pyroclastic displays of chthonic vigor. Earth endlessly erases what was and provides a blank slate for what is to come.

And then there is the final departure of every form of life on Earth brought to us courtesy of our old friend Mr. Sun, the traitor. The sun will survive for another ten billion years, but in five billion years it will turn into a Red Giant whose reach will extend beyond the orbit of Mars, incinerating the inner planets. But don't get too comfortable because in just one billion years, the sun's brightness will have increased by 10 percent, evaporating the oceans and making Earth uninhabitable, just another of the universe's abundance of drifting rocks.

∽

That's the big stuff. But for humans there is something subtler than the kind of death we associate with corpses: dead dog here, tiger there, Aunt Hazel in her calico dress over yonder. It is something more personal and melancholy. It is this: If you live long enough, you will see the human world into which you were born disappear. The conditions and the worldly forms into which you were born and which you had taken to be perdurable reality will "suffer a sea-change into something rich and strange." You will look about, confused, like a person who "hath lost his fellows/And strays about to find 'em," as Shakespeare imagined in *The Tempest*.

Many of the things that disappear will be gone and good riddance. Other things, the things we loved, we will watch wistfully, elegiacally, as if we were seeing yet another disappearance of Praxiteles's statue "Resting Satyr," his mocking eyes sinking beneath a rising tide of mud.

I'm seventy years old and the world that I grew up in is almost lost to sight. As I say, a lot of that is for the good, but, for me, it is quite another matter if the arts, and the possibility of transcendence that the arts provide, are on a list of vanished things.

The arts were not my birthright. I grew up in a working-class suburb in the San Francisco Bay Area at a fortunate time when public education was good, college was affordable (cheap actually), and few students graduated with debt. And so it was possible for me to sally forth without the threat of young adult bankruptcy. Since I wasn't worried about a job just then, and I was accustomed to being poor, I was free to be something else, an English major at the University of San Francisco. A student of the classical guitar up the hill at Lone Mountain College. A longhair war resistor and draft counselor in the chaplain's office. There seemed to be no limit to the wonderful things I could be in order to make it unlikely that I'd ever cross paths with money. I was poor, but it felt like I was thriving, and I wasn't the only one with that feeling.

But in the present, things have undergone a sea change that is strange enough but not at all rich. The university, the university as I knew it, no longer exists. In the age of neoliberal austerity, programs in the arts and humanities have been reduced or removed because budgets are tight and computers come first, or there is no "student demand," or, crassly, there is no market for what the arts have to offer. What's lost in such market logic is the fact that programs in the arts and humanities—not just in universities but at all levels of education—are the primary way in which we are introduced to fundamental questions about who we are, where we are, how we got here, and what, if anything, we'd like to see changed. These are lofty purposes for education, but with each passing decade they seem to be pushed ever further from view. Instead, we have what David Harvey described succinctly: "The traditional university culture, with its odd sense of community, has been penetrated, disrupted, and reconfigured by raw money power."[2]

II.

> I will not serve that in which I no longer believe
> whether it calls itself my home, my fatherland, or
> my church.

—*James Joyce*

In spite of the near death of the liberal arts in academia, I will continue to think of myself as a citizen of the humanities because when I was a student who had rejected all the forms offered to me by nation state, capitalism, and family, I found a home with a warm hearth in the study of literature. In this home I felt that I had been returned to what the German idealist philosopher Friedrich Schiller called an "original power," or Nature, something like what Buddhists call Buddha Mind. And in this home, I felt for the first time a freedom from the goals and desires that defined the world around me.

For me, the humanities still have an aura of welcome and benevolence. After all, the arts never claimed to know it all. From the Renaissance forward, the arts have been about discovery, not certainty. More importantly, as the epigraph from James Joyce declares above, art has mostly developed at a hostile angle to the reigning platitudes of any given time. The great masters of oil painting were subversive because what they portrayed was more real than what their traditions had allowed to that point, more real in all sorts of ways, including the abstractions of Cézanne and then Kandinsky. And they were subversive because they were ever more stylistically adventuresome, offering a model of freedom to their audiences, something no structure of power is comfortable with.

As art critic John Berger wrote:

> Each time a painter realized that he was dissatisfied with the limited role of painting as a celebration of material property and with the status that accompanies it, he inevitably found himself struggling with the very language of his own art as understood by the tradition of his calling.

Perhaps Berger was thinking of someone like Goya, whose court portraits often subtly mocked the nobility's self-importance and vanity, and whose use of color and texture anticipated the Romantic revolution so near at hand. Or Egon Schiele's stark self-portraits, like *Seated Male Nude*, which he created even after the state sentenced him to six weeks in jail for obscenity.

When I imagine that the artistic subversions I have admired and learned from are no longer of any consequence, I feel like I'm part of that place Yeats wrote of: "No country for old men." I feel alien. A social isolate. As Italo Calvino wrote in an elegiac mood, my mood, "The world had changed: I couldn't recognize the mountains any more, or the rivers, or the trees." This, too, is impermanence, the fading of the beautiful.

❧

Perhaps I should accept that the arts, too, are subject to impermanence, but that doesn't make witnessing their fading any less disturbing. For example, I was recently giving a reading at Fifty-Seventh Street Books in Chicago and a man of about my age came up to me afterward and said, "I admire your work, but it occurred to me that you are writing for a world that no longer exists." Or, as a wag later put it to me in a comment on the *Lapham's Quarterly* website, "You're so last century."

In the age of climate disruption, plague, and looming nuclear disaster (the Doomsday Clock moves imperceptibly forward each year as if in one of Zeno's paradoxes) even the concept of "future" feels like something from a lost world. "Concern for the future?" we ask. "What future?" Perhaps in some not-so-distant time—"after the human game has played itself out," in Bill McKibben's words—every writer and poet who has ever lived, even the worst of the hacks, will be, perversely, as famous as Shakespeare. Which is to say that every artist known and unknown will be sunk in the same mire, like so many creatures and curiosities of the Jurassic, in a tar pit of our own making.

III.

There is a secret stream of art and ideas that moves through the popular. As a young man, I didn't feel that going to the Fillmore for the pleasures of psychedelia was a project separate from going to San Francisco Symphony Hall to hear von Karajan conduct Beethoven. After all, these days some of our folk music, the *vox populi* inside popular music, is self-knowing and complex in a way we used to expect only of "serious" music. For example, one of Radiohead guitarist Jonny Greenwood's influences, especially for his film scores, is the modernist composer Olivier Messiaen. And pianist Keith Jarrett composed one of the most beautiful jazz works that I know, *Survivors Suite*, and followed it with a radiant recording of Shostakovich's *Preludes and Fugues*. And cinema, at its best, has realized Richard Wagner's dream of the "total work of art": music, image, and story in one organic whole, as in the films of *Nouvelle Vague* directors Jean-Luc Godard and Agnes Varda, or New German Cinema directors Rainer Werner Fassbinder and Werner Herzog. Lars von Trier's *Melancholia* is utterly aware of itself as a total work of art, beautifully employing Wagner's music and imagery throughout.

So, I must have been wrong to think I'd lived long enough to see my world die. Only the ephemera has arisen and passed, gone like a neon Sign of the Flying A from a long-vanished gas station, while my world, both secret and canonical, has endured—in a word, in a note, in a brush stroke.

I assume this is good news, but why is it good news? The arts endure, but what is it that endures? Why does it endure? Is it only because of its subversive powers? Important though those powers are, I have come to think not. As I said earlier, the first thing art offered me was the warmth of the living, a refuge, and a consolation. It offered me the "feeling-tone" of a wisdom indistinguishable from beauty.

This is the feeling that John Berger describes while standing "wordless" before Rembrandt's *A Woman Bathing in a Stream.** Berger takes part in the artist's wonder at the intimacy of the human body, and at the way the body becomes a channel for spirit. As Berger writes of this painting, it is the "rediscovery as if for the first time of a familiar body." But this body is not the product of the culpable male gaze; it is the product of a loving gaze that is, wonderfully, not separate from what it sees. The artist discovers himself gathered together with his subject, this living flesh, and they are gathered in the collective unfolding of the world. As Zen master Dogen expressed it, "Enlightenment is the intimacy of all things." Rembrandt leaves the tradition of painting-as-theology for a place that is wiser than theology. This is not merely a famous image to be checked off a life list before moving on to the next famous image. Instead, the work provides living access to an old meaning. Like Buddha nature, this meaning is present if we can see through the crust of the customary to Rembrandt's awakened heart.

It is not the painting itself that allows this awakening, the thing that collectors covet, the thing that has a price tag at auction of $50 million, and it is not the trite idea that it is a masterpiece or a work of genius or a part of the history of the development of style. Rembrandt had none of this in mind when he made this painting. He was bankrupt. He

---

* See Rembrandt van Rijn, *Woman Bathing in a Stream* (1654), oil on panel, National Gallery of England, London UK. View at: https://www.nationalgallery.org.uk/paintings/ rembrandt-a-woman-bathing-in-a-stream-hendrickje-stoffels

painted for himself. He painted in order to mend a world that had fallen about his ears. He wanted to create an image of light emerging from darkness, his understanding of what is unchanging, undying, always here and now. Rembrandt is famous for his many self-portraits, and, in a sense, this is a self-portrait. Rembrandt puts on his Original Face. He has come to rest. Nothing remains to be done. We honor this moment when, like Berger, we stand wordless, or mindful, before it.

Rembrandt's fellow bankrupt, Jan Vermeer, sought a similar awakening in his painting *A Woman Holding a Balance.*[*] An otherworldly expression on her face, a woman holds an empty scale. Before her are two strings of pearls. The pearls suggest the transience of worldly goods, but in their luminescence they also suggest a beyond, a domestic *Sacré Coeur*. Distracted from the calculation of wealth, she experiences a moment of transcendence, a moment out of time. The pearls are both the problem and the solution. It is as if Vermeer were saying that we don't have to seek spirit out there somewhere; it is always right here, even in the little world of the household, waiting to be recognized.

Vermeer captures the moment of the woman's recognition, her sudden awakening. Imagine the painting without

[*] See Jan Vermeer, *Woman Holding a Balance* (1662–63), oil on canvas, National Gallery of Art, Washington DC. View at: https://www.nga.gov/collection/art-object-page.1236.html

the pearls, with a stack of money instead. Without the pearls, and without the delicate transition of shade into light on the wall behind her, the painting would still be masterful, but it would have a more didactic meaning—the triviality of worldly things in the face of the Last Judgment (which hangs on the wall behind the woman). Instead, the woman and her pearls invite us to contemplate a little theophany, an unexpected descent of the divine, and to linger in its aura.

In the *Lotus Sutra*, Dharma refines the Three Vehicles, the three thousand realms, and the ten thousand things to a single thought-moment. Like this clarifying gesture, Vermeer refines the thousands of brushstrokes, the layers of studies and drawings beneath the surface of the painting, his teachers and their influence, the masters who influenced his teachers, and the whole history of Western painting as the search for spiritual insight, to a single thought-moment.

As Master Dogen imagined: "One bright pearl is able to express reality without naming it."

∽

Or consider Gerard Manley Hopkins's poem "God's Grandeur." First, he offers the fact of the matter, what we find in the world. We find that "The soil is bare now," and that our roots lack rain.

> *All is seared with trade; bleared, smeared with toil;*
> *And wears man's smudge and shares man's smell.*

In spite of the debasing of the world by humans, the ultimate terms of which we are seeing now, Hopkins then tells us "there lives the dearest freshness deep down things" that cannot be "bleared." But this freshness is not only in things; it is also in the poem itself. The poem shares in God's grandeur. The poem is never a dead thing, part of a world that no longer exists. It is like a musical note that decays only to be returned to life by the next note that decays only to be once again redeemed. The artist "lets go" of realist representation and joins the play of energy in the void. The artist is the maker of worlds, breaker of worlds, maker of worlds, and again breaker, in what Nietzsche called the "eternal return."

For Hopkins, when art is worthy of our care, it cannot die. It cannot die because, like Vermeer's pearls, it is a facet of what is "deep down things." It is part of what Buddhism calls an Original Brightness, ever emerging. Of course, this could all be Romantic yearning after an experience of something that only exists *as* yearning. It could be that it does not provide eternity but only the "artifice of eternity," as William Butler Yeats called it. Which is not to say that if it is artifice it is therefore false. Perhaps it is exactly artifice—the arts, spiritual traditions, peak experiences of nature, even science's revelations about the nature of the cosmos—that provides our access to the transcendent.

In the late eighteenth century, after the work of artists and poets was relieved of the requirement to flatter money and power, and was free for the first time (free to go hungry in too many cases), there were many artists like Hopkins who sought personal spiritual renewal. In the first half of the twentieth century, there was Wallace Stevens's poem

"Of Mere Being" with its "palm at the end of the mind," in which a "gold-feathered bird sings" and its "fire-fangled feathers dangle down." Or Yeats's "Sailing to Byzantium," where Grecian goldsmiths create forms of hammered gold to "set upon a golden bough to sing."

But the question remains: "What is it that endures in what the painters, the musicians, and the poets have shown us?" There is no confusion for Hopkins. What endures is the brightness of God's grandeur, "shining like shook foil." But these are truly deep matters, and they exist, for most of us, on the other side of a gap. The practice and the experience of art offers access to this other side through that unknowable thing we call beauty. Similarly, Buddhism shows us that this gap can be crossed through meditation, attention, and awareness. We awaken to what is on the other side of this gap, even if, on most days, we only get up from our cushions muttering about our backs.

For most of us, the experience of a beyond is fleeting and uncertain, and we meet it with a pause. It's like Dante's "Final Vision" in the *Paradiso,* where he sees what he has sought: "One Simplicity of Light." The sweetness of this moment is like what one "sees in dream, and when the dream is gone an impression, set there, remains," but just the impression. Dante's earthly powers "fail the deep imagining," until, happily, the next heartening appearance of "the Love that turns the Sun and the other stars."[3]

Epilogue: Our Last ~~Fact~~

∞

I don't worry 'bout a thing, 'cause I know
nothing's gonna be all right.

—Mose Allison

For me, Buddhism's most endearing quality is its happy
gloom. No other religion is so certain that nothing can be
fixed, certainly not the "world," whatever that is. And no
other religion is so insistent that the bedrock of life is *samsara*, suffering and change.

But there are stranger things than this. The next turn
of the Dharma Wheel suggests that suffering is our teacher.
Without *samsara*, the suffering and change and ignorance that
so easily make their way among us, there would be nothing
to wake from, and thus no possibility of transcendence. But
it's hard to be grateful for such teachers when there are so
many of them, beginning with the ancient triad of aging,
sickness, and death. On top of that are piled capitalism's
banal cruelties, poverty, racism, gender bigotry, colonialism,
nationalism, militarism, authoritarianism of left and right,
the slouching beast of environmental catastrophe, and, most

recently, the Dostoyevskian fatalism of Vlad Putin's nuclear extortion in Ukraine, because of which I cannot know in this moment if the sentence I'm writing will ever be read. And all of this is the eternal consequence of the Three Poisons—greed, anger, and delusion—driven by the demonic mentality that Randy Newman described well in his song "Old Kentucky Home":

> *I got a fire in my belly*
> *And a fire in my head*
> *Goin' higher and higher*
> *Until I'm dead.*

That's Trumpism (and so many other awful things) in brief.

So, yes, that's the gloom for sure, but what's the happy part? The happy bit is that although there are Three Poisons, there are also Three Jewels: the teacher (Buddha), the teaching (Dharma), and the community of students (Sangha) for all of which we should be duly grateful. But there is a caveat to the happiness provided by the Jewels, because these two groups of three are not opposed to each other, as if it were a case of sin versus virtue, or good versus bad. They do not exist in opposition because, in the parlance of *The Heart Sutra*, they are "empty of self-existence." Instead, they are codependent: happygloom, perhaps. Without the Poisons, there would be no Jewels, and no need for a Buddha, his wisdom, or his community.

So, it's not only suffering that we need to be released from;

it's also happiness and the struggle for whatever we think will make us happy, including the ambition to become enlightened. Buddhism offers something beyond suffering and happiness. Some call it Ultimate Truth, but let's call it Our Last ~~Fact~~. Our Last ~~Fact~~ is that there is no suffering and no happiness, no *samsara* and no nirvana, and no truth and no falsity. There is only either fetters or freedom from such contested terms, only enslavement to or release from our "fixed views" of what is good or bad, true or false. For Shunryū Suzuki, the realization of Our Last ~~Fact~~ is itself the end of suffering:

> When we hear that everything is a tentative existence, most of us are disappointed; but this disappointment comes from a wrong view of man and nature. It is because our way of observing things is deeply rooted in our self-centered ideas that we are disappointed when we find everything has only a tentative existence. But when we actually realize this truth, we will have no suffering.

This is the genius of the Middle Way, and it is what makes Buddhism a religion and not just a precocious form of philosophic skepticism. Contrary to what Stephen Batchelor imagines, Buddhism is not a religion because of its metaphysics or its magical thinking about an infinity of Buddhas and flying bodhisattvas, mantras, and tantras. It is truly a religion because it seeks to provide release from belief in either poison or jewel, suffering or happiness. Buddhism is a religion because it is about transformation, as in the hymn "Amazing Grace": "I once was lost, but now I'm found."

In *Emptiness,* Frederick Streng's 1967 study of the second-century C.E. Indian philosopher Nagarjuna, he describes Buddhism's religious impulse as "the way of release":

> [Nagarjuna] stands within the Buddhist tradition that begins the religious discussion with the general human situation of incompleteness and frustration. . . . The person who accepts the emptiness-teaching regards life's sorrows as his own construction and knows that he must desist from constructing them in order to be released. . . . The awareness of emptiness provides this freedom in that objects or forces which make an absolute claim on the individual are seen as empty. As this awareness grows, there is a continual process of detachment from these claims and an expansion of awareness. This is a freedom which applies to every moment of existence, not to special moments of mystical escape to another level of being . . . [Emptiness provides] a radically salutary power by which man is saved from himself.

We, too, can experience Nagarjuna's salvific release in any moment in which we recognize the instability in what we had assumed was firm substance. The English poets called this recognition "mutability." As Percy Bysshe Shelley wrote:

> We are as clouds that veil the midnight moon;
> How restlessly they speed and gleam and quiver,
> Streaking the darkness radiantly!

And so a tree is not a "thing" because it is rooted only in change, as in Piet Mondrian's *Apple Tree in Blossom*.* The whole of creation flows through the trunk of this apple tree as if its being were at the intersection of multiple currents purling in the tree's heartwood and then flowing up through branch, blossom, and fruit. Knowing this doesn't require irrational belief, it only requires caring enough to look in those ways that spiritual teachers like Nagarjuna, poets, musicians, and painters have encouraged us to look in order see what F. Scott Fitzgerald called art's "high white notes," when the work of art transcends itself and becomes an expression of spirit's freedom. Through this freedom we find the Buddha's release from self-inflicted suffering, and we also find art's promise not of happiness but of honesty, its offer of refuge, its promise to reveal to us "what is."

Yet, one might object, isn't this freedom just indifference? What about evil, what about the petroleum industry, what about domestic Fascists, and what about utterly unenlightened beings like Donald Trump and Putin? Shouldn't we confront them? Indeed, we should! Thich Nhat Hahn's "engaged Buddhism" begins exactly here where freedom from suffering becomes one with freedom from fear. As he

---

* See Piet Mondrian, *Apple Tree in Blossom* (1912), oil on canvas, Kunstmuseum de Haag, the Hague, Netherlands. View at: https://www.kunstmuseum.nl/en/collection/ flowering-apple-tree

wrote in his "Fourteen Precepts of Engaged Buddhism," "Have the courage to speak out about situations of injustice, even when doing so may threaten your own safety."

The end of suffering is the beginning of courage.

Beyond those moments when there is no option other than confrontation, what Naht Hahn called for was the creation of enlightened, principled, and brave communities— like his own Plum Village, in southern France. Seen from the world we actually live in, a demon's slapstick notion of the good life, Plum Village looks like just another grand illusion. In our world, after all, pertinacious clowns like Trump and Putin cruise in top-down Mercedes, waving Stetson hats overhead and hootin' and hollerin' like Slim Pickens riding the Big One to Earth in *Dr. Strangelove*.

In spite of all the murderous comedians around him, Naht Hahn persisted in building a thriving spiritual countercul-ture in what the Tibetan Wheel of Life calls the Realm of the Human. But while we know that that realm can grow larger, as indeed it has, it is unlikely ever to entirely displace darker realms, especially the Realm of the Gods, the oli-garchs, court jesters with blood on their hands. Plum Vil-lage is an expression of Naht Hahn's commitment to human community. It is a sort of demonstration community, a spiri-tual subdivision outside of the City of Money.

Refuges like Plum Village may be as close as we deeply damaged beings will ever come to nirvana. But as jazz Arkestra leader Sun Ra once said, "Heaven is where you'll be when you are okay right where you are!"

Acknowledgments

Above and beyond type, thanks to Dennis Johnson, Valerie Merians, Carl Bromley, and the rest of the Melville House crew past and present for ten years of full-throttle fun. Loud shout-outs to James Shaheen and Andrew Cooper at *Tricycle* for imagining I had something to say that had something to do with Buddhism, and to Lewis Lapham for his always spirited support.

"Living in a World that No Longer Exists" originally appeared in *Tricycle*.

"Freedom: It's Not About You" and "Beyond Money: Living in a World Without Stars," originally appeared in *Lapham's Quarterly*.

"California Karma" and parts of "Beyond Money: The Samadhi of the Collective" originally appeared in *Salon*.

"Wagner's Passion" originally appeared in *The Rupture.*

"Living in a World Without Stars" originally appeared in *Lapham's Quarterly.*

"Boss Trump" originally appeared in *MobyLives.*

A short section of "Beyond the Database Buddha" originally appeared in an earlier book, *We, Robots: Staying Human in the Age of Big Data* (2015).

Primary sources.

For "Wagner's Passion":
Jonathan Carr, *The Wagner Clan: The Saga of Germany's Most Illustrious and Infamous Family* (2009), and Joachim Köhler, *Richard Wagner: the Last of the Titans* (2001).

For "Music's Music":
Henry-Louis De La Grange, *Mahler: A Biography.*

Endnotes

Prologue

1 Musicians like Glenn Gould, Jimi Hendrix, and John Coltrane are a new thing, the musician/creator. Just listen to Coltrane's "Naima," or the guitar solo on Hendrix's "Little Wing." Gould playing the *Goldberg Variations* is self-explanatory. All hail!

2 Or maybe it is all about the brain since the brain depends on the intestines to create neurotransmitters like serotonin, and the intestines depend upon the consumption of plants and animals, and the plants and animals depend upon soil and sun, and soil and sun . . . etc. As Zen master Dogen taught, "I came to realize clearly that mind is nothing other than rivers and mountains and the great wide earth, the sun and the moon and the stars." This is Indra's jewel-strewn net of life.

3 Ironically, Yamamoto Tsunetomo, author of *Hagakure*, agreed, "It is bad when one thing becomes two. One should not look for anything else in the Way of the Samurai. It is the same for anything that is called a Way. Therefore, it is inconsistent to hear something of the Way of Confucius or the Way of the Buddha, and say that this is the Way of the Samurai. If one understands things in this manner, he should be able to hear about all Ways and be more and more in accord with his own."

4 In spite of my criticisms here, Schrader's three-part *Transcendental Style* is still a helpful way to read some contemporary Asian cinema. For example, Jia Zhangke's *The World* (2004) is set in Beijing World Park, a sort of Disney World of international icons (the Eiffel Tower, pyramids, etc.) where the employees live in dormitories. This is the "everyday." This utterly alienated everyday becomes "disparity" through the unhappiness of two lovers who feel trapped in the park and unable to fulfill their relationship. However, "stasis" is perverse: the film ends with the lingering image of the two lovers lying unconscious on the street outside a friend's apartment, perhaps dead from natural gas asphyxiation. Even Shohei Immamura's serial killer flick *Vengeance Is Mine* (1979) has a "stasis" shot in the last scene: there is a "frozen view" of the bones of the executed killer hanging in midair after his father flings them off a mountaintop. The Zen imaginary survives in these films, but it has no relationship to Zen itself. See also, Bi Gon's extraordinary *Long Day's Journey into Night* (2018) with its closing stasis shot of two sparklers burning down.

5 At the beginning of an Idles concert, lead singer Joe Talbot will present the audience with his own form of *metta* practice, "Be kind or get the fuck out!" It's all compassionate mayhem after that.

Beyond the Database Buddha

1 Comically, this is a familiar riddle for science that physics calls the "observer effect"; the disturbance of an observed system by the act of observation.

2 See Donald Lopez's *The Scientific Buddha: His Short and Happy Life*, 2012, for a full historical and critical account of Buddhism and science.

3 I adapt the idea of social "ecologies" from Owen Flanagan's *The Geography of Morals: Varieties of Moral Possibility*, 2012.

4 "Corporations Are Trying to Co-opt Mindfulness to Avoid Meeting Worker Needs," *Truthout*, June 5, 2021.

5 "The Land of Many Dharmas," *Tricycle*, Summer 2021.

6 Of course, the counterculture also had at least one science hero, Einstein, in part because of his pacifism and in part because he seemed to say to science "everything you know is wrong," which was very much the mood of the moment. Quantum physics also had its appeal in books like Fritjof Capra's *The Dao of Physics*, Robert Pirsig's *Zen and the Art of Motorcycle Maintenance*, and Gary Zukav's *The Dancing Wu Li Masters*.

7 The neurobiologist Semir Zeki attempted a similar neuro-dissection on art. Zeki used brain scans to analyze what areas of the brain determine whether something is beautiful. Zeki asks, "Can an aesthetic judgment ever be quantified? The answer is yes." (*Inner Vision: an Exploration of Art and the Brain*, 1999). I suppose this could be called the neuroscience of the Beauty Spot.

8 "Davos: Mindfulness, Hotspots, and Sleepwalkers," *Huffington Post Blog*, March 28, 2014.

9 Michelle Ye Hee Lee, "Hitting Mung: In stressed-out South Korea, people are paying to stare at clouds and trees," *The Washington Post*, November 21, 2021.

10 "On Doing One's Utmost in Practicing the Way of the Buddha," *Shobogenzo,* Hubert Nearman, editor, Shasta Abbey Press, 2007.

11 Thich Naht Hahn and Daniel Berrigan, *The Raft is Not the Shore*, 1975.

12 See "What the Buddha Thought," an interview with Richard Gombrich in *Tricycle*, Fall 2012.

13 *Ultimate Concern: Tillich in Dialogue*, Harper and Row, 1965.

14 "The Unfamiliar Familiar," *Tricycle*, Fall 2014.

15 Roger R. Jackson, "Review: Stephen Batchelor's *After Buddhism*," *Lion's Roar*, January 29, 2016.

16 (1) There is suffering/dissatisfaction (*dukkha*); (2) the cause of dissatisfaction is the Three Poisons: anger, greed, and delusion; (3) there is an end to dissatisfaction in wisdom; and (4) there is a way to wisdom through the Eightfold Path.

17 "Regret: A Love Story," *Tricycle*, Winter 2019.

18 *In the Buddha's Words: An Anthology of Discourses from the Pali Canon*, 2005.

19 Quoted in Johan Hari, "Unable to Concentrate," *The Guardian,* January 2, 2022.

20 "Apple and Amazon's big lie: The rebel hacker and hipster nerd is a capitalist stooge," *Salon*, March 8, 2014.

21 *Columbus and Other Cannibals*, 1979.

22 From a Dharma talk by Andrea Fella, Insight Meditation Center in Redwood City, CA.

23 It's worth noting here that Buddhism's most famous Western advocate Alan Watts first studied Buddhism at the London Buddhist Lodge founded by Theosophists in the 1920s.

24 The idea that Western Buddhism employed Romanticism as a "gate" to the Dharma is not entirely novel. Scholars like David McMahan (*The Making of Buddhist Modernism,* 2008) have studied this influence, and then there is Thanissaro Bhikkhu's "The Roots of Buddhist Romanticism" (*Purity of Heart*, 2012). Bhikkhu argues, as I would, that German Romanticism, especially Schiller, created an intellectual context that eventually allowed Buddhism to seem familiar in the West. However, he tends to see psychology (Jung) and psychotherapy as the primary beneficiaries of this connection, not poetry and the arts. You might also notice that Bhikkhu's work is very much "precariously on the margins of society," as Conze noted, and not in an academic department of religious studies. The essay is in a volume published by the Metta Forest Monastery.

25 Translation by Benjamin Sher.

26 In Hegel's language, we have moved from the merely in-itself (the unconscious boy), to the for-itself (the awakening poet), to the in-and-for-itself, being and knowing as one.

27 In the philosophical parlance of the time, Wordsworth is describing *natura naturans*, nature as self-developing activity, or "nature naturing." Philosophers and poets of the age thought of their work as a part of the becoming of Nature.

28 See Herbert Marcuse's sublime interpretation of Hegel's Absolute as the infinity of "play." The Absolute is "free self-externalization, release, and 'enjoyment' of potentialities"; it is "sensuousness, play, and song" (*Eros and Civilization*, 1955).

29 Stephen Mitchell translation.

30 "Scientists' egos are key barrier to progress," Ian Sample, *The Guardian*, September 10, 2021.

31 See Stuart Ritchie's 2020 book *Science Fictions: Exposing Fraud, Bias, Negligence and Hype in Science* for the grimy details.

Beyond Money

1 You may recall Col. Jack D. Ripper's thoughts on a similar matter in Stanley Kubrick's *Dr. Strangelove*, "Fluoridation is the most monstrously conceived and dangerous communist plot we have ever had to face. . . . A foreign substance is introduced into our precious bodily fluids. . . . That's the way your hard-core Commie works."

2 See also Mark Carney's Reith Lectures: "How We Get What We Value," for a similar market-positive vision of moral reform.

3 Samuel Stebbins, Grant Suneson, "Jeff Bezos, Elon Musk among US billionaires getting richer during coronavirus pandemic," *USA Today*, December 1, 2020.

4 See Marx, "Conversion of Surplus-Value into Capital," "The ever repeated purchase and sale of labour-power is now the mere form; what really takes place is this—the capitalist again

and again appropriates, without equivalent, a portion of the previously materialized labour of others, and exchanges it for a greater quantity of living labour."

5 "Amazon Has Turned a Middle-Class Warehouse Career into a McJob," Matt Day and Spencer Soper, December 17, 2020.

6 "California Water Futures Begin Trading Amid Fear of Scarcity," Kim Chipman, *Bloomberg Green*, December 6, 2020.

7 In Woody Allen's *Blue Jasmine*, Jasmine (Cate Blanchett), a socialite down on her luck, finds herself outside of her special realm and living in her sister's spare bedroom. She is bewildered and, like any animal out of its element, terrified.

8 "Did Trump Deliberately Pursue Genocide via His 'Herd Immunity' Strategy?" *Truthout*, December 17, 2020.

9 "SYSOUT=A," *The Review of Contemporary Fiction*, Spring 1996.

10 "Dying from corona virus: A Tyson worker family's final goodbye," Annette Cary, *Tri-City Herald*, April 22, 2020.

11 *Culture of Death*, 1885.

12 *The Spirit in the Gene*, 1999.

13 "The *Lancet* Commission on Pollution and Health," October 19, 2017.

14 "Can Psychedelics Treat Climate Grief," *The Guardian,* April 23, 2020.

15 From the movie *Coconuts* (1929), the year of the Great Wall Street Crash.

16 In late April 2020, Las Vegas and Phoenix registered five consecutive days of record heat of 100–115 degrees. This was accompanied by record lows in the high 70s.

17 *Bankei Zen*, translated by Peter Haskel (1984).

18 Quoted in the *New York Times* obituary for Grau, August 11, 2020, written by Katharine Q. Seelye.

19 "Corona Virus: the Journey to In-between," Sacred Mountain Sangha Blog, April 27, 2020.

20 From www.rdwolff.com/faq.

21 Marx wrote his doctoral thesis on Epicurus.

22 "Marxism, Prefigurative Communism, and the Problem of Workers' Control," *Radical America*, #11, 1977.

23 Rodrigo Toscano, "'Blood,' 'Spirit,' and 'Nation' Stuff: A Dialogue Between Rodrigo Toscano and Julie Carr," *Big Other,* April 28, 2021.

24 *Truthout*, May 27, 2021.

California Karma

1 See Robert Lustig's Web lecture "Sugar: the Bitter Truth" for the bitter truth. (University of California TV)

Boss Trump

1 Ask Rick Perry how this works. Trump blamed Perry for his notorious phone call to President Zelensky of Ukraine, commenting disingenuously, "Not a lot of people know this, but I didn't even want to make the call. The only reason I made the call was because Rick asked me to." In the aftermath of January 6, even his shock troops, the Proud Boys, were abandoned.

2 Actually, Randolph was a lot like Trump. Wikipedia has this to say about him: "Like many Old Virginia Conservatives, Randolph believed that the purpose of government was to empower men like him. Empowered by the Virginia government, Randolph believed that gentry such as himself should rule over all those beneath him, including farmers, women, and enslaved African Americans. Like many members of the Virginia gentry, Randolph despised democracy, preferring a form of republican government that favored white men born into wealthy, prominent families."

Wagner's Passion

1 Baudelaire appears to have been similarly charmed. He wrote fan mail to Wagner, including this orgasmic passage: "I experienced a sensation of a rather bizarre nature, which

was the pride and the joy of understanding, of letting myself be penetrated and invaded—a really sensual delight that resembles that of rising in the air or tossing upon the sea."

2 See especially his essay "David Strauss: the Confessor and the Writer" from Nietzsche's first book *Untimely Meditations*. Nietzsche argues that the true German nation should be united under "one style," Wagner's style, as he makes clear in the volume's last essay, "Richard Wagner in Bayreuth."

3 In Nietzsche's last sad dementia, the ravenous spirochetes of syphilis having nibbled away one too many cerebral nerve root, he was heard to ask about his "wife, Cosima Wagner." His last letter was to Cosima: "Ariadne, I love you. Dionysus."

There is, out in that great blasphemous reflection of all things us-like, YouTube, an eerie and heartbreaking kinetograph of the twilight Nietzsche in various states of addled repose. In one scene, a woman (his anti-Semite sister Elizabeth?) sits at his side reading a book. In another, a large bug seems to climb up his arm.

Music's Music

1 *The Music Lesson: A Spiritual Search for Growth Through Music*, Victor L. Wooten, 2006, Penguin/Random House.

2 From *Concerning the Spiritual in Art*, Wassily Kandinsky, 1977.

3 Mahler is usually thought of as the last romantic, but this anecdote shows him to be a modernist. As Kandinsky put it, "That art is above nature is certainly no new discovery." See Theodor Adorno's *Mahler: a Musical Physiognomy* for a full treatment of Mahler the modernist.

4 Listen to the hemidemisemiquavers in the contrabass in the second movement of Beethoven's Eighth Symphony. In F major, if you're wondering about what key farts are played in. (Apologies to Mike Judge's movie *Office Space*.)

5 *The New Yorker*, April 7, 2021.

Living in a World that No Longer Exists

1 "The Taste for Nothingness," from *Les Fleurs de Mal*, trans. James McGowan.

2 "University, Inc." *The Atlantic*, October, 1998. A review of Bill Reading's *The University in Ruins*, 1997.

3 Translation A. S. Kline.